The Conflict Resolution Process

The **Conflict** Resolution Process

A Consultant's Handbook

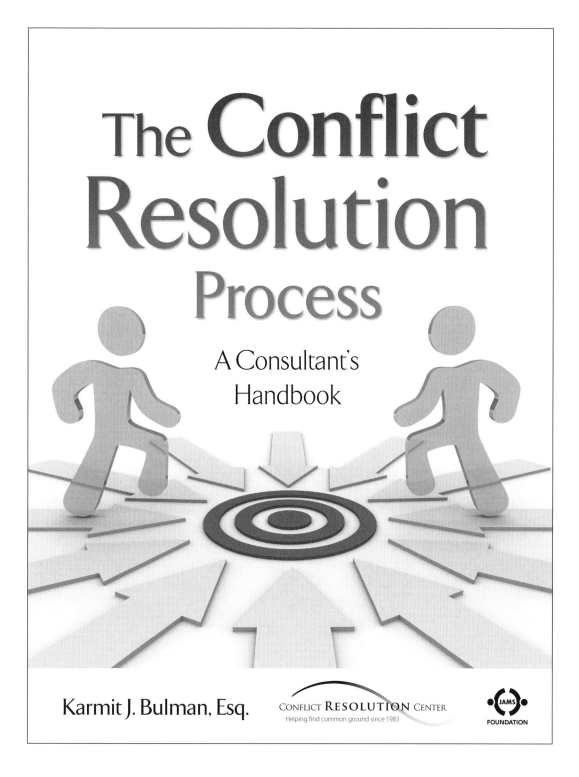

Karmit J. Bulman, Esq.

CONFLICT **RESOLUTION** CENTER
Helping find common ground since 1983

JAMS FOUNDATION

BEAVER'S POND
PRESS

ISBN: 978-1-59298-469-5

Library of Congress Control Number: 2012904871

Book design by Ryan Scheife, Mayfly Design

Typeset in Adobe Caslon Pro, Univers, and Triplex

Printed in the United States of America

First Printing: 2012

16   15   14   13   12   5   4   3   2   1

Beaver's Pond Press, Inc.

7108 Ohms Lane

Edina, MN 55439-2129

(952) 829-8818

www.BeaversPondPress.com

To order, visit www.BeaversPondBooks.com

or call (800) 901-3480. Reseller discounts available.

Contents

Chapter One

What is Conflict Resolution Consulting?

Conflict is prevalent in every aspect of life. Conflict is present wherever there are people, ideas, feelings, and beliefs. Try as we may to escape it, or wish it away, it is an integral part of who we are. What sets us apart as human beings is the complexity of our thoughts, our ability to remember vivid details from the past, and the vision to imagine our future. We have strongly held beliefs, values, and ideas; we have notions of what is right and what is wrong; and we seek truth, justice, and equality. It is because of all this that conflict is ever present.

Think of a truly juicy conversation you might have recently had with a friend or loved one. Chances are you were analyzing, dissecting, or processing a conflict. Perhaps it was a disagreement, misunderstanding, tension, or dilemma. Conflict can move us forward, move us to a new stage of development, or it can tear us apart. Most of us do not receive conflict resolution instruction, and our skills are minimal. The material in this book is for those who find themselves in the position of regularly helping others turn crisis into opportunity. This means mediators, counselors, friends, and people helpers of all varieties. While many of

> "Conflict is present wherever there are people, ideas, feelings, and beliefs."

the chapters are structured for people helpers to formally assist those in conflict, the information can be used by those who find themselves having regular conflict or communication difficulty with friends, coworkers, or relatives.

When disputants call a mediation program for assistance in resolving a conflict, they have taken a bold step. All too often, however, one party refuses to come to the table. Due to the absence of one party at a scheduled mediation session, participants may leave without having had the opportunity to talk through their situation and receive assistance in the management of their dispute. When one party does not show up for the mediation, the mediator scheduled for the session should, if she or he feels comfortable, approach the party who is present and ask if he or she would like to meet one on one to discuss the reason for the mediation and brainstorm possible solutions. In addition, many people who call for mediation assistance feel hopeless and unsure where to turn when they request mediation, and then discover that the other party will not participate. In those situations where mediation is not an option, conflict resolution consulting is a valuable option. It is an opportunity for anyone who would like to resolve a nagging issue or conflict to do so in a proactive, productive, and meaningful way.

How does it work?

When a person is in a conflict, many different routes are available to help resolve the conflict. While some methods are legal processes, such as litigation, many, such as negotiation, mediation, and arbitration, are not. Each option has benefits and drawbacks. Negotiation can be described as a simple back-and-forth process where only the impacted parties are involved. Mediation is much the same, only the meeting is facilitated by a neutral party. Arbitration is a more regimented process between the parties, where a neutral third party issues a binding decision when the process concludes. Litigation is the traditional legal process, highly regimented, where a judge issues a binding decision at the end of the hearing.

These options—negotiation, mediation, and arbitration—are arranged in order of least expensive to most expensive and also by processes most driven by the parties themselves to the processes least driven by the parties. For those familiar with the legal system, using arbitration or litigation can be a good route to use their skills. For the rest of us, however, the legal system is often stressful and confusing and the decisions often seem arbitrary. The biggest complaint from those who take the legal route is frustration about never getting to "tell their story." Though decisions that come from the legal realm have a higher chance of being followed, as they are binding, parties coming from a well-run negotiation or mediation are more likely to follow their own agreement. This makes sense, as people are more inclined to follow an agreement in a process where they felt they were heard and had a say in the outcome.

In this spectrum, conflict resolution consulting falls between negotiation and mediation. Conflict consulting teaches the skills necessary for a good mediation, such as good listening and good communication; however, this involves a meeting with only one invested party. Participants are able to explore a conflict they are embroiled in and develop their own constructive strategies and action plans. They are given the opportunity to further develop skills and consider tactics that may help them move toward a solution. The consultation takes place in a private and confidential setting and participants are encouraged to be honest and open in exploring possible solutions. Conflict resolution consultation can be used in almost any dispute and can help the participant achieve clarity about what the next steps might be in moving toward a solution.

Conflict resolution consulting provides a systematic, three-level program that assists a person in conflict to express emotion, develop strategies to move constructively forward, and create a conflict resolution action plan. It is important to note that this process is not coaching, counseling, therapy, or advocacy. Rather, conflict resolution consulting can be described as a form of mediation, facilitated with only one disputant present, with the mediator acting as a neutral party, as in traditional mediation.

Often when a disputant is in a conflict, it is not feasible, desirable, or practical for the other side in the dispute (i.e., adversary) to be present for a mediation session. Many potential participants leave mediation centers without receiving conflict management assistance because of this. While some mediation programs provide informal one-on-one sessions with participants, conflict resolution consulting has not been systematized to any great extent. Consequently, mediators have not been professionally prepared for, or trained in, working with disputants in this model of dispute management.

The Conflict Resolution Center (CRC) of Minneapolis, with assistance from the JAMS Foundation, has developed a comprehensive system and program enabling mediators and other people helpers to serve as conflict resolution consultants. Conflict consulting provides space for participants to share their feelings and perspectives about the dispute with a trained consultant. The process can be broken down into three components: emotional expression, skills-building, and action planning.

Emotional Expression

Allowing the party to vent feelings and relate experiences is a very important aspect of the consulting session. Emotional expression about the conflict can provide a disputant with a sense of empowerment and can also serve as an opportunity for the participant to more objectively reflect on the situation. In venting related emotions, the participant can also clarify and better understand some of the underlying issues of the conflict.

Skills-building

During a consulting session, the participant has an opportunity to learn some new tools and skills that can be used both with the absent party and in other conflicts. The consultant can use the session to rehearse possible communications the participant might have with the other party, to prepare the participant for mediation, and provide coaching in successful communication skills for use in any action plans formulated during the session.

Action Planning

During this final stage of the consulting session, the consultant may guide the participant in developing strategies, brainstorming solutions, and using tools such as reality testing and conflict mapping. During this stage, the participant can be provided with referrals, and the consultant may discuss ways to encourage the other party to come to a mediation session.

Who can be a conflict resolution consultant?

A conflict resolution consultant needs training. The most effective basic education for this role is mediation training. As mentioned before, mediation is an informal process in which a neutral third party assists the parties to reach a voluntary resolution of a conflict. Mediation gives the parties the opportunity to discuss issues, clear up misunderstandings, determine the underlying interests or concerns, find areas of agreement, and, ultimately, to incorporate those areas of agreements into resolutions. A mediator is impartial and facilitates a process so that the participants can come up with their own resolution.

The mediation process is strictly confidential and participation is voluntary. Conflict resolution consultants use the same skills as mediators and should conduct consulting sessions that are confidential and neutral and focus on the self-determination of the participant. The basic premises of mediation apply in conflict resolution consulting sessions. Consultants do not take sides, give advice or information, or tell the participant what to do. Consultants are impartial and neutral as they assist the participant in developing their own plans. In addition to basic mediation skills training, consultants need at least a two-day workshop that covers the many components of a conflict resolution consulting session, in addition to training on conflict resolution skills development, conflict management, and theory.

> "Consultants do not take sides, give advice or information, or tell the participant what to do."

In addition to basic mediation skills, an effective consultant will do the following:

- Establish conflict as "normal" for the party.
- Serve as a process consultant to assess the situation and select an appropriate conflict management style or strategy for approaching the other person.
- Help the party think through how to approach the other person, what to say, and how the other person might respond.
- Focus on conflict management rather than on recommending outcomes.
- Help develop a plan for addressing the conflict constructively.
- Give the disputant an opportunity to practice what he or she will say when addressing the other person involved in the conflict.
- Offer affirmation and encouragement.

(Adapted and printed with permission from Good Shepherd Mediation Program Conflict Resolution Coaching 2009 Training Manual)

What will happen at the consultation?

A consultation generally lasts about two hours, but more time or additional sessions can be arranged, if necessary. The consultant begins the session by affording the participant an opportunity to share the reason for coming to the consultation. Questions such as "What do you need?" and "What do you want the other person to know?" might be asked of the participant. The consultant will help identify the participant's most important needs. The participant will also be asked to consider the needs of the other person involved in the conflict.

After the participant has explored the perspectives, needs, and interests involved in the conflict, the consultant assists the participant in identifying what skills and understanding may be helpful to develop before working toward a solution. The consultant may rehearse possible discussions with the other person, prepare the participant for an upcoming mediation, or concentrate on successful communication skills for working toward resolution of the conflict. This process is designed to help the participant understand how he or she typically deals with conflict and to consider the most productive ways to respond.

After a period of time in which the participant works on skills and understanding of conflict, he or she may choose to explore different options to resolve the issues. The consultant helps the participant to arrive at appropriate next steps. Consultation may not be a final solution to the conflict, but will help the participant thoughtfully and carefully develop steps that can move it in the right direction. By identifying what the needs and issues are for the participant in this consultation, considering the other party's concerns and needs, and exploring solutions to each issue that meet both parties' concerns, a plan for a lasting solution may be reached.

Chapter Two

Understanding Conflict

What is conflict?

If it is possible to define conflict in simplistic terms, we might suggest that conflict is behavior in which people oppose one another in their thoughts, feelings, or actions. There are always three key ingredients in a conflict: thoughts, feelings, and action. Meanings, judgments, and values crowd our minds and move us to conflict. Feelings are underneath, and are an important dimension of conflict. For example, anger, hostility, fear, jealousy, insecurity, pain, sadness, and/or inadequacy are some of the feelings underneath conflict. Finally, all conflicts have an action component—some external behavior is exhibited such as body movements, facial expressions, or speaking.

Obviously, relationships are a key component of conflict. One might even suggest that where there are two or more human beings involved, there will be conflict. Good relationships have two basic required skills: communication and compromise. Each of these is a means to handling conflicts; without good skills in these areas, conflict is unavoidable.

So where does conflict come from? It arises from a clash of goals or values involving a concern where people care about the outcome.

Simply put, if you didn't care, you wouldn't have a conflict. It can start with confusion or disagreement about a common objective and how to achieve it. It can be exacerbated when people feel that their core concerns are not being met. Core concerns are discussed in detail in Chapter Eight.

"We study conflict because life is full of paradox. When we allow two or three different ideas to be true all at once, we are exercising first-rate intelligence. When opposing ideas enter into our consciousness or conversation, and we are able to juggle all these ideas without 'dropping' the most inconvenient ones, we make ourselves resilient and adaptable to life's challenges. Holding onto paradoxical thinking means you can help mediate conflict in groups, families, and the world. People who feel compelled to rush to judgment contribute little to conflict resolution. People who accept that many things are true at once add to the world's store of sanity."[1]

Types of Conflict

As summarized by Christopher Moore in the Mediation Process and on the website of the Oregon Mediation Center,[2] conflict can be evaluated according to five categories: relationship, data, interest, structural, and value.[3] By determining the causes of a conflict, it may be easier to design resolution strategies that will have a higher probability of success.

> "By determining the causes of a conflict, it may be easier to design resolution strategies that will have a higher probability of success."

1   William Wilmot and Joyce Hocker, *Interpersonal Conflict* (New York: McGraw Hill, 2001), 7.

2   Christopher Moore, *The Mediation Process* (San Francisco: Jossey-Bass, 2003, 60–62) and http://www.internetmediator.com/medres/pg18.cfm (Accessed February 2012).

3   Ibid.

Relationship Conflicts

Relationship conflicts occur because of the presence of strong negative emotions, misperceptions or stereotypes, poor communication or miscommunication, or repetitive negative behaviors. Relationship problems often fuel disputes and lead to an unnecessary escalating spiral of destructive conflict. Supporting the safe and balanced expression of perspectives and emotions for acknowledgment (not agreement) is one effective approach to managing relational conflict. On top of this, the varying types of relationships—from parent/child, to friendships, to relationships between significant others—all give rise to different inherent power balances and different criteria for what a successful resolution would be. Being aware of the nature of a particular relationship and what this means for the conflict can be critical to achieving a satisfactory result.

Data Conflicts

Data conflicts occur when people lack information necessary to make wise decisions, are misinformed, disagree on which data are relevant, interpret information differently, or have competing assessment procedures. Some data conflicts may be unnecessary since they are caused by poor communication between the people in conflict. Other data conflicts may be genuine incompatibilities associated with data collection, interpretation, or communication. Most data conflicts will have data solutions.

Interest Conflicts

Interest conflicts are caused by competition over perceived incompatible needs. Conflicts of interest result when one or more of the parties believes that in order to satisfy his or her needs, the needs and interests of an opponent must be sacrificed. Interest-based conflict will commonly be expressed in positional terms (meaning people will assert their position). A variety of interests and intentions underlie and motivate positions in negotiation and must be addressed for maximized resolution. Interest-based conflicts may occur over *substantive* issues (such as money, physical resources, time, etc.), *procedural* issues (the way the dispute is to be resolved), and *psychological* issues (perceptions of trust, fairness, desire for participation, respect, etc.). For an interest-based dispute to be resolved, parties must be assisted to define and express their individual interests so that all of these interests may be jointly addressed. Interest-based conflict is best resolved through the maximizing integration of the parties' respective interests, positive intentions, and desired experiential outcomes.

Structural Conflicts

Structural conflicts are caused by forces external to the people in dispute. Limited physical resources or authority, geographic constraints (distance or proximity), time (too little or too much), organizational changes, and so forth can make structural conflict seem like a crisis. It can be helpful to assist parties in conflict to appreciate the external forces and constraints bearing upon them. Structural conflicts will often have structural solutions. Parties' appreciation that a conflict has an external source can help them jointly address the imposed difficulties.

Value Conflicts

Value conflicts are caused by perceived or actual incompatible belief systems. Values are beliefs that people use to give meaning to their lives. Values explain what is good or bad, right or wrong, just or unjust. Differing values need not cause conflict. People can live together in harmony with different value systems. Value disputes arise only when people attempt to force one set of values on others or lay claim to exclusive value systems that do not allow for divergent beliefs. It is not useful to try to change value and belief systems during relatively short and strategic mediation interventions. It can, however, be helpful to support each participant's expression of his or her values and beliefs for acknowledgment by the other party.

Conflict and Relationships

The rational course of conflict changes depending upon the nature of the relationship between the parties. A conflict stemming from a parent-child relationship should be handled differently from an intimate relationship or an employer-employee relationship. The following will outline some strategies and considerations for conflicts between parties in specific relationships.

Parent/Child Conflict

With a parent/child relationship, the association is involuntary and there are power and resource imbalances that may be necessary for a healthy relationship, especially early in a child's life. When this is combined with the necessity of caring for the proper development of the child, this type of conflict presents a fundamentally different situation, which should be handled with care. One of the first things to dismiss is the idea that the parent's inherent ability to hold the majority of power and resources within the relationship means that conflict is to be viewed solely as a child disobeying a parent's control. It is generally preferable to identify conflict with a wider lens, namely something that is an inevitable consequence of humans regularly interacting with each other rather than something that is by definition always the fault of one party.

Note that nearly all conflict resolution skills that children possess are gained directly or, more likely, indirectly, from the parents. Children grow up watching and learning and, eventually, mimicking their parents' techniques, whether discussing, coercing, avoiding, fighting, compromising, or other. As such, even if discussing and bargaining are not a parent's preferred method of dealing with conflict, it can be useful to point out that in the future it would be useful to attempt to only use these methods around their children if they are the methods they would like the child to use to handle the inevitable conflicts that will arise in the future. A parent who slaps a child and loudly yells, "Be quiet and don't hit your brother!" is unlikely to impart skills of cooperative discussion-based conflict resolution to his or her child.

Employer/Employee Conflict

An employer/employee conflict is unique and difficult in that it also has power imbalances, which should be respected if the employee wishes to continue being employed. However, these power imbalances are not always healthy. Therein, the challenge is how to work around the power imbalances, rather than how to undo or address them. Along with this, as hinted at earlier, work conflicts have the ability to become much more stressful than other types of conflicts, especially during a hard economy, as people are unwilling to "rock the boat" and risk losing their jobs, and therefore will put up with a minor conflict until it reaches a critical point.

Intimate Relationship Conflict

In an intimate relationship conflict, such as that between romantic partners or family members, emotions play a substantial role. As such, emotional expression and feeling heard are critical. It is not uncommon for the majority of the problem to be solved once the party unloads his or her emotions and has some time for clarity. The key to solving emotional conflicts is getting the parties to discuss emotional issues in a nonemotional manner. Conflict resolution consulting might be very helpful in the intimate relationship arena. Having a chance to vent to an impartial consultant, feeling heard by another and being given a chance to sort out next steps, might be critical to restoring a relationship and providing for growth. It is also often necessary to look at how past misunderstandings or interactions may have crept into how each family member feels about the other. In resolving intimate relationship conflict, letting go of the past and seeing what is possible for the future is a crucial component for resolution.

Friendship Conflict

Conflicts within friendships present a different set of circumstances. Issues of trust, dependability, and values clarification are common themes in conflicts between friends. This is largely because we expect (and not unreasonably so) that our friends will always be our allies and confidants; and it is rare that two people will have the same viewpoint on everything, even if they are good friends. Conflict can, however, be beneficial to a friendship; once discussed and clarified, conflict can strengthen a friendship. Even though most of us pursue friendship because of the enjoyment, satisfaction, and growth involved, this does not mean friendships have fewer conflicts than other relationships. A strong friendship will have conflict. Friends usually choose to work through and resolve the conflict, avoid it and keep the friendship going, or allow the friendship to end. Without the legal bonds, connection to financial security, or status, many people don't expend the energy to resolve friendship issues. Sometimes an issue such as money owed becomes the primary conflict between the parties; once the disputants discuss what is at the heart of the matter, however, it becomes clear that friendship is what needs to be addressed, not money.

Conflict and Identity[4]

"Most people are in conflict because they believe someone or something is preventing them from being 'who they are' or 'who they want to be.' Likewise, people in conflict are often ignorant of how their actions are negatively impacting the identity of the other." Identity can be defined as a person's framework for "who they are" or "who they want to be." There are many types of identity:

- Personal. These include attitudes, values, character, ethnicity, gender, race, age, and the like.
- Professional. Work and organizational-related roles have significant meaning to us.
- Situational. A certain situation may make us a leader, follower, victim, joiner, or peacemaker, and may give us a status we closely identify with.
- Relational. We may be a spouse, parent, sibling, neighbor, or coworker, and our feelings about our identity change in each of these roles.
- Cultural. Our heritage, nationality, work culture, race, religion, ethnicity, age, gender, birth order, and many other cultural factors are interwoven and contribute to our identity.
- Organizational. Every organization (military, nonprofit, corporate) has its own culture, and this provides each participant with a related identity.

---

4   Adapted and printed with permission from Good Shepherd Mediation Program Conflict Resolution Coaching 2009 *Training Manual.*

The "Face" Metaphor

Face is a metaphor for how we self-identify.[5] When our identity is threatened, there is likely to be conflict; consider the phrases "losing face" or "shamefaced." People in conflict may feel that their face is threatened. Certain words from others, actions or interactions, may threaten people's desired identity or make them feel their capacity, strength, reputation, or status has been diminished. As the conflict escalates, people become increasingly invested in saving face and are less likely to consider another person's claims of face. "Threats to face may result from perceptions of public humiliation, personal disregard, unjustified intimidation, insults, patronizing airs, and contemptuous offers."[6]

Conflict consultants help participants explore identity issues by discussing how to manage their "face" needs and those of the other (e.g., how to enhance face, protect face, repair face, save and protect face for all concerned). Consultants can help participants gain emotional clarity around who they are and who they want to be seen as or respected as. It is helpful to participants to examine their self-image, status, and role with regard to other people.

Attitudes about Conflict

Conflict is one of the most pervasive aspects of human affairs. It exists in almost all relationships, whether personal or organizational, formal or informal. Conflict is almost universally regarded in negative terms. It is viewed as something to be avoided and feared. There is a widespread attitude of hopelessness and helplessness in coping with conflict. When conflict cannot be contained in a functional way, it can erupt in argument, destruction, violence, and war. The harmful aspects of conflict are

---

5   Erving Goffman, "On Facework: An analysis of ritual elements in social interaction," *Psychiatry Journal of Interpersonal Relations*, 18:3. 1955. 213–214.

6   Douglas H. Yarn, "Conflict Consulting." *Dictionary of Conflict Resolution* (San Francisco: Jossey-Bass Inc., 1999), 175.

obvious. Death and physical harm are apparent consequences of unresolved conflict. Less obvious is the psychological damage to individuals, loss of productivity on the job, destruction of relationships, organizational breakdowns, and other devastation.

Conflict has many benefits as well. Kenneth Cloke, author of numerous books on conflict resolution, defines conflict as "an indicator of a need to make a transition to a new state and an opportunity to develop new skills to evolve to that new state." Conflict can motivate people to act and break them out of complacency. Sometimes conflict is necessary to bring an awakening to dysfunctional relationships or behavior. Conflict can be a source of growth in organizations, communities, and societies, and can lead to positive changes and new relationships. "Conflict serves the function of 'bringing problems to the table.' In intimate relationships, conflict can make clear that there are problems to be solved. Conflict often helps people join together and clarify their goals. Conflict can also function to clear out resentments and help people understand one another."[7]

Stages of Conflict

Generally, conflict builds through four stages—discomfort, incident, tension, and crisis—although it can begin at any one of the stages. The earlier a conflict is identified and dealt with, the easier it is to resolve. Stage one is the discomfort stage. At this stage, there is nothing concrete to identify what has happened, but a tuned-in person might have a vague intuitive feeling that something is not right. During stage two, the incident stage, something minor might happen that leaves one or both parties feeling irritated or upset, but it might be ignored or considered not worth bothering about. When these incidents are ignored, they tend to simmer quietly and, later, other incidents are added to it.

7   Wilmot and Hocker, 15–16.

During this stage, misunderstandings may arise from poor communication, lack of rapport, cultural differences, or personality variations. If left alone, misunderstandings may snowball until tension surfaces.

By stage three, the tension stage, it is apparent to everyone that something is amiss. The people involved in the conflict may try to enlist others to support them, and partisan groups may form. The relationship becomes weighed down with negative feelings, and parties begin to characterize the other party as rude, disrespectful, untrustworthy, manipulative, and a host of other blame-based adjectives. If action toward resolution is not taken during stage three, crisis will flare up. By stage four, the crisis stage, the relationship has totally broken down; any semblance of normal behavior between the parties will have disappeared. The parties may hurl insults at one another, gossip harmfully about the other, show extremes of emotion, or resort to violence. Often at this stage, one party or the other leaves the relationship completely. While it may be possible to rebuild the relationship at this stage, this is an unlikely outcome. The damage may seem irreparable, or the parties have decided that they don't care.

> "The earlier a conflict is identified and dealt with, the easier it is to resolve."

A conflict can move backwards through the stages if a complete resolution is not reached. Unless completely resolved, a small conflict that reappears will escalate due to the baggage carried from previous incidents. As stated earlier, resolving conflicts during stages one or two are critical to relationship recovery.

Parties to conflicts have three basic options for resolving or altering conflicts:

1. *Try to change the other party.* This is rarely successful. Parties in conflict usually believe they have good reasons for their viewpoints and position. You can influence the other party. If there is a power differential between the parties, the more powerful person is likely to get his or her way. However,

"power-over" tactics usually lead to fear and resentment, which are unhealthy dynamics in any relationship.

2. *Try to change the conflict conditions.* If you can increase scarce resources, change perceptions of incompatible goals, or make some other change in the conflict elements, you might be able to resolve the conflict. Changing the structure of a conflict is desirable; however, it is not always possible.

3. *Change your own communication and/or perceptions.* "This is usually the most difficult, and paradoxically, the most successful way to resolve conflict. Changing what you do and think about the other party will quickly and profoundly affect the conflict elements in the relationship. You change before the other person changes."[8]

Transforming conflict usually requires at least one of the parties to change his or her perceptions or reframe some of the underlying concepts involved. The way different people perceive things is at the core of most conflicts. "In interpersonal conflicts, people react as though there are genuinely different goals, there is not enough of some resource, or the other person is getting in the way of something prized by the perceiver. Sometimes these conditions are believed to be true, but sorting out what is perceived and what is interpersonally accurate forms the basis of conflict transformation."[9] Effective conflict resolution "requires effective communication, or expression of the conflict, checking one's perceptions, and transforming the elements of the conflict. Our connections with other human beings, while a source of conflict, also allow us the opportunity to forge new relationships that are growth producing."[10]

Once the nature of the conflict has been identified, it is often useful to break it down into its various elements: the people, the process,

---

8   Ibid., 219.

9   Ibid., 41.

10 Ibid., 62.

and the problem contained within a conflict. This helps both identify where the conflict is coming from and what is necessary to ensure that the conflict is truly resolved.

People

The people within a conflict are all of the parties involved in the conflict. This might include friends, family, neighbors, coworkers, community members, and others directly or indirectly impacted by the conflict. Understanding the history, values, and personalities of the parties is essential, as well as recognizing the emotion we all carry. To explain and justify our feelings is a characteristic need of being human.

Process

The process behind a conflict is simply the manner in which the parties address the conflict, such as the procedure and guidelines for communication. A good process should empower all parties, feel fair, and deal with any potential power imbalances that the parties bring to the conflict. Cultural nuances influence what process is chosen to resolve a conflict, as do lack of resources, such as money, time, knowledge, transportation, and other factors.

Problem

Lastly, the problem is obviously the substance of the conflict. When analyzing this component, think about not only the facts of the situation, but also about underlying perceptions and interests driving the conflict. If they are not explicitly stated, it is worthwhile to take some time attempting to uncover these underlying driving forces. It is a good idea to restate and clarify these perceptions and interests as they are being expressed.

Sources of Conflict

In order to become truly adept at handling conflict, we must not only solve conflicts as they arise, but understand where conflict comes from. If we are able to comprehend the different origins of conflict and can see how various forces can then exacerbate or calm the conflict, we can become much better conflict resolution consultants. Not only will we be able to grasp the true nature of the conflicts, but we will be able to help participants tailor solutions that address the exact sources this conflict arises from.

Approaches to Conflict

Three approaches to solving conflict are available to the parties of a dispute: power-based, rights-based, or interest- or need-based approach.

Power Based

A power-based approach to solving conflict works by determining which party has more power in the relationship. Whichever party had the most power would then win the conflict. This approach can be seen in most violent confrontations, such as war.

Rights Based

The next approach is rights based. A rights-based approach focuses on a separate set of rules that both parties are bound by to weigh the position of both parties. This approach can be found most commonly in litigation or arbitration, where a standard set of laws is applied dispassionately to a situation to resolve it.

Interest/Needs Based

The last approach is an interest/needs-based approach. In this approach, the parties first state the positions and the desires they bring to the table. The parties then identify the interests and needs that underlie these positions. These interests and needs are often much more pivotal to resolving the actual conflict than their originally stated positions, on top of being more conducive to reaching an agreement than their uncompromising original hard-line desires.

Needs are at the center of most conflicts; frequently people believe their needs are inconsistent with those of others. "Needs are imbedded in a constellation of other forces that can generate and define conflict. In order to effectively address needs, it is usually necessary to work through some of the other forces that can generate and define conflict. There are five basic forces or sources of conflict: the ways people communicate, emotions, values, the structures within which interactions take place, and history."[11]

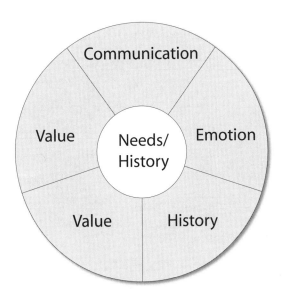

Bernard Mayer, *The Dynamics of Conflict Resolution,* San Francisco: Jossey Bass, 2000, 8–9.
Reproduced with permission of Jossey Bass (John Wiley & Sons, Inc.),

11 Bernard Mayer, *The Dynamics of Conflict Resolution,* San Francisco: Jossey Bass, 2000, 8–9.

The Nature of Needs

In a needs-based approach to conflict resolution, we look into the nature behind people's needs. Psychologist Abraham Maslow developed a hierarchy of needs, which can be seen in Figure 1. Maslow's theory revolved around the idea that there is an ordering of needs, and that people only move to address higher needs when their more basic needs are already satisfactorily addressed.

This hierarchy is organized as follows: (1) physiological; (2) security and safety; (3) love and feelings of belonging; (4) competence, prestige, and esteem; (5) self-fulfillment and the need to understand. While obviously as humans we have the ability to act and think in a much more complex way than any such straightforward theory, there is still great truth to the idea that we give less importance to higher-level desires when our more fundamental needs are being threatened. As such, it is necessary to keep Maslow's theory in mind when identifying what a person's interests and needs are in a given conflict, to make sure that conflicts are solved on the best level. This framework helps us focus on the underlying needs as a pathway to create a win-win solution. Without it, solutions tend to be win-lose, where only one side's true issues are solved, or even a lose-lose, where neither side walks away with a solution.

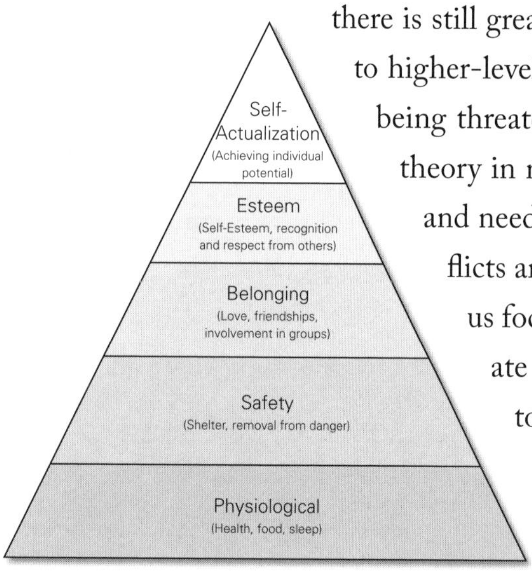

Fig. 1. Maslow's Hierarchy of Innate Needs

List of Needs

Connection	Physical Well-Being	Autonomy
acceptance	air	choice
affection	food	freedom
appreciation	movement/exercise	independence
belonging	rest/sleep	space
cooperation	sexual expression	spontaneity
communication	safety	
closeness	shelter	**Meaning**
community	touch	awareness
companionship	water	celebration of life
compassion		challenge
consideration	**Honesty**	clarity
consistency	authenticity	competence
empathy	integrity	consciousness
inclusion	presence	contribution
intimacy		creativity
love	**Play**	discovery
mutuality	joy	efficacy
nurturing	humor	effectiveness
respect/self-respect		growth
safety	**Peace**	hope
security	beauty	learning
stability	communion	mourning
support	ease	participation
to know and be known	equality	purpose
to see and be seen	harmony	self-expression
to understand and	inspiration	stimulation
be understood	order	to matter
trust		understanding
warmth		

Fig. 2. © 2005 by Center for Nonviolent Communication. Reprinted with permission.

Chapter Three

The Physiology of Conflict

Our bodies are programmed to respond to stress automatically, meaning we have a system in place that reacts and adapts to stressors unconsciously. This system is the autonomic nervous system and is composed of the sympathetic and parasympathetic nervous systems. These two branches of the autonomic nervous system are like the gas pedal (accelerator) and brake pedal (decelerator) of our body. The sympathetic nervous system (accelerator) is more commonly understood as the "fight or take flight" system. This is an archaic circuit that was designed to keep us alive in the event of a life-threatening situation.

In extreme situations, such as if you are hiking in the woods and stumble across a bear cub and the mama bear jumps out after you to protect her baby, the sympathetic nervous system is stimulated. The goal is to either prepare your body to fight or take flight, meaning that you are going to either fight for your life or run for your life. So what happens in the body's physiology (function) to allow this to occur? Think about it in a very simplistic way; if you were going to run for your life (or fight for your life), you would want the majority of your blood flow to be shunted away from certain organs (like your stomach, intestines, and kidneys) and directed to your muscles, heart, and lungs. You would need your airways within your lungs (bronchioles) to dilate, allowing for increased oxygen exchange. The heart rate and blood pressure would need to rise to increase blood circulation through your body. Your pupils would dilate, too, allowing more light to enter the eye for enhanced vision. On top of all that, a variety of endorphins (hormones) release into the bloodstream to alter pain and other sensory perceptions. These reactions occur instantaneously and without conscious thought; think about being startled and how quickly your heart rate increases.

The example above is hopefully an unrealistic situation, but these same changes and body responses occur even in smaller forms of stress. Being stuck in traffic, having an argument or fight, the pressure of personal and professional deadlines to meet, and even walking up a small flight of stairs can trigger the response of the sympathetic nervous system to varying degrees within the body. Depending on the intensity of duration of the stressor(s), these physical changes will vary in their effect on the body and even mental function, which will be discussed later in this chapter.

The complement or counter to the sympathetic nervous system is the parasympathetic nervous system. The parasympathetic nervous system is the other branch of the autonomic nervous system, which slows the body down, rather than preparing for a fight or take flight reaction. It's involved in slowing respiration rate and heart rate, lowering blood pressure, constricting the pupils, stimulating repair, and increasing activity and blood flow to the digestion and urinary systems, along with other functions that allow the body to rest and repair. Just like the sympathetic nervous system, these actions of the parasympathetic nervous system happen without any conscious thought. Typically after meals and during the evening is when your parasympathetic nervous system is most active.

Just as a car is not functional with only a gas or brake pedal, nor is your body. It's the balance between the sympathetic and parasympathetic nervous systems that allows us to function healthfully and efficiently throughout the day. Being consistently stimulated in only the sympathetic or parasympathetic is not beneficial. There is a delicate balance between the two that is consistently being monitored and adjusted according to the internal and external environment.

What component of the autonomic nervous system is stimulated more often in your body throughout the day? Odds are, if you're like the average American, you said sympathetic nervous system. We are exposed to a tremendous amount of physical, mental, and chemical stressors daily that our bodies are constantly responding to and thus our sympathetic nervous system is activated to varying degrees.

So how does the autonomic nervous system relate to conflict engagement? In any conflict, an individual wants to make rational decisions and have rational reactions while effectively communicating with the other party. Unfortunately, a large percentage of individuals do just the opposite: they become irrational, acting and speaking aggressively, which they later regret. At one point, we've all looked back on how we handled a situation and wondered, "What was I thinking?" Even an individual who is normally very rational can act extremely irrationally within a conflict or stressful situation. What's going on to allow this behavior to occur?

When it comes to making decisions, actions, and choices, two regions of the brain are primarily responsible: the rational brain (prefrontal cortex) and the emotional brain (limbic system/amygdala). The

> "At one point, we've all looked back on how we handled a situation and wondered, 'What was I thinking?'"

rational brain (prefrontal cortex) controls a vast amount of functions, including social and personal behavior, making choices between right and wrong, assessing conflicting thoughts and options, problem solving, rational thought and assessment, complex thought and analysis, and much, much more. On the other hand, the emotional brain (limbic system/amygdala) controls emotional and primitive reactions that are typically immediate, and usually far more aggressive than what the initial stressor or trigger should have elicited.

It would seem obvious that the rational brain should be activated during a conflict or argument, but unfortunately that normally doesn't happen. When the body perceives stress (physical, emotional, and/or chemical), as discussed earlier, the sympathetic nervous system and emotional brain are highly active. This is key, because an active emotional brain disrupts the function of the rational brain (prefrontal cortex); a highly emotional reaction can lead to a lack of inability to think rationally. When we have done something we later regret, we probably were thinking with our emotional and not our rational brain.

In Daniel Goleman's book *Emotional Intelligence: Why It Can Matter More Than IQ*, he coined the term "amygdala hijacking."[12] Basically this is our emotional brain taking over and limiting the function of our rational brain. According to Goleman, amygdala hijacking happens when the body is stressed or perceives threats (sympathetic nervous system activation) and this input bypasses the rational brain and is sent directly to the emotional brain. During this situation, one's reactions (physical and mental) are instantaneous, exaggerated, and more intense than what the initial stimulus calls for.

So how does this come back to conflict, and engagement within it? It comes down to an obvious question: Would you prefer to be in conflict with an individual reacting with a rational brain or an emotional brain? Take a moment and think about a situation where you experienced an amygdala hijacking—where you or someone else completely overreacted to a relatively minor situation. Would you want to interact with that individual? For most individuals, conflict and engagement within it is a very stressful event easily triggering the sympathetic ner-

---

12 Goleman. *Emotional Intelligence: Why it can matter more than IQ* (New York: Bantam, 1995), 13–32

vous system and the emotional brain. This can cause a disruption in rational thinking, behavior, and communication for any individual, and escalate any conflict or even possibly stimulate amygdala hijacking of the brain.

What can you do? There are a few techniques that are useful in overcoming the triggering of the emotional brain and reengaging the rational brain. The first step and key concept is recognizing that you or someone else is in a sympathetic nervous system and emotional brain state of activity. Recognition is absolutely necessary to combat this situation, but at times it is extremely difficult to be aware of this reaction in yourself. Mediators within mediations will often perform a reality check of the situation, and you can do the same with your emotions. Perform an emotional check of yourself; ask yourself questions such as, "What emotion am I feeling?" and "Am I responding in a rational or emotional way?" If you find yourself or someone else to be more emotional-brain activated, here is what you can do:

A. Take a time-out or break, giving yourself and others a cooling-off period. For some individuals, this can take up to fifteen minutes before the intense response of the emotional brain ceases.

B. If taking a time out is not possible, focus on your breathing. Taking slow deep breaths can decrease the effects of the sympathetic nervous system and emotional brain.

C. Wait five to ten seconds before you respond to a question or statement. Give your rational brain a chance to assess the situation. The emotional brain reaction is typically instantaneous, so if you can fight the urge to respond right away, you'll limit that emotional brain response.

Another powerful technique is to label feelings within yourself and/or other individuals. Neuroscientist Lieberman stated that, "putting feelings into words (affect labeling) has long been thought to help manage negative emotional experiences," and his research indicated, "Affect labeling, relative to other forms of encoding, diminished the response of the amygdala and other limbic regions to negative emotional images."[13]

Lieberman summarized these findings extremely well in an interview by the UCLA College of Letters and Science: "When you attach the word 'angry,' you see a decreased response in the amygdala," Lieberman said. "When you attach the name 'Harry,' you don't see the reduction in the amygdala response."

"When you put feelings into words, you're activating this prefrontal region and seeing a reduced response in the amygdala," he said. "In the same way you hit the brake when you're driving when you see a yellow light, when you put feelings into words, you seem to be hitting the brakes on your emotional responses."[14]

The body is always in a state of responding to stressors, small or large, consciously or unconsciously. Being aware of these responses and the changes in your body will give you an advantage in any situation, especially within conflict engagement. The difficult aspect is being able to recognize this behavior in yourself and others and, once recognized, taking the appropriate measures to limit the effects of the emotional brain. Biofeedback therapy and techniques are a great resource to develop conscious awareness of the sympathetic nervous system and its effects.

---

13 M.D. Lieberman, et al. "Putting Feelings Into Words: Affect Labeling Disrupts Amygdala Activity in Response to Affective Stimuli." *Psychological Science*, 18(5), 2007, 426.

14 UCLA College of Letters and Science. "Putting Feelings Into Words Produces Therapeutic Effects in the Brain." 2007. http://www.college.ucla.edu/news/07/feelings-into-words.html (Accessed February 2012).

Chapter Four

Helping Others Transform Their Conflict

As a society, we tend to avoid disputes. We think of them as costly and unnecessary, requiring only brief attention. Conflict, however, if addressed in a positive fashion, can be an overwhelmingly beneficial process. If it were not for scientists such as Galileo, who sought conflict with society to prove that the earth was not the center of the universe, our society would not have continued to advance. The challenge then becomes how best to ensure that our conflict-resolving methods are positive ones that propel the situation forward.

Conflict Resolution Styles

In the 1970s, Kenneth Thomas and Ralph Kilmann[15] asserted that "conflict situations are those in which the concerns of two people appear to be incompatible." They identified five main styles of dealing with conflict that vary in their degrees of cooperativeness and assertiveness. In

---

15 Modified and reproduced by special permission of the Publisher, CPP, Inc., Mountain View, CA 94043 from Thomas-Kilmann Conflict Mode Instrument by Kenneth W. Thomas and Raqlph H. Kilmann. Copyright 1974, 2002, 2007, 2012 by CPP, Inc. All rights reserved. Further reproduction is prohibited without the Publisher's written consent."

such situations, an individual's behavior can be described along two basic dimensions:

A. Assertiveness, the extent to which the person attempts to satisfy his or her own concerns, and

B. Cooperativeness, the extent to which the person attempts to satisfy the other person's concerns. These two basic dimensions of behavior define five different modes for responding to conflict situations:

  1. *Competing* (think of a shark) is assertive and uncooperative—an individual pursues his or her own concerns at the other person's expense. This is a power-oriented mode in which we use whatever power seems appropriate to win our own position—our ability to argue, our rank, or economic sanctions. Competing means standing up for our rights, defending a position that we believe is correct, or simply trying to win.

  2. *Accommodating* (think of a teddy bear) is unassertive and cooperative—the complete opposite of competing. When accommodating, the individual neglects his or her own concerns to satisfy the concerns of the other person; there is an element of self-sacrifice in this mode. Accommodating might take the form of selfless generosity or charity, obeying another person's order when we would prefer not to, or yielding to another's point of view.

  3. *Avoiding* (think of a turtle) is unassertive and uncooperative—the person neither pursues his or her own concerns nor those of the other individual. Thus the conflict is avoided. Avoiding might take the form of diplomatically sidestepping an issue, postponing an issue until a

better time, or simply withdrawing from a threatening situation.

4. *Collaborating* (think of an owl) is both assertive and cooperative—the complete opposite of avoiding. Collaborating involves an attempt to work with others to find some solution that fully satisfies their concerns. It means digging into an issue to pinpoint the underlying needs and wants of the two individuals. Collaborating between two persons might take the form of exploring a disagreement to learn from each other's insights or trying to find a creative solution to an interpersonal problem.

5. *Compromising* (think of a fox) is moderate in both assertiveness and cooperativeness. The objective is to find some expedient, mutually acceptable solution that partially satisfies both parties. It falls between competing and accommodating. Compromising gives up more than competing but less than accommodating. Likewise, it addresses an issue more directly than avoiding, but does not explore it in as much depth as collaborating. In some situations, compromising might mean splitting the difference between the two positions, exchanging concessions, or seeking a quick, middle-ground solution.

Each of us is capable of using all five conflict-handling modes. None of us has a single style of dealing with conflict. But certain people use some modes better than others and, therefore, tend to rely on those modes more heavily than others—whether because of temperament or practice. Our conflict behavior is therefore a result of both our personal predispositions and the requirements of the situation in which we find ourselves.

> "None of us has a single style of dealing with conflict"

Models of Conflict Behavior[16]

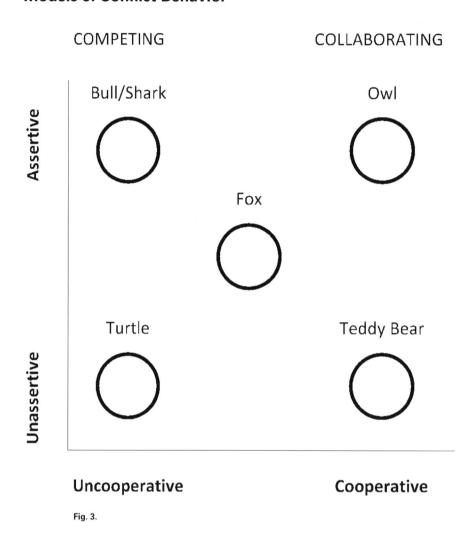

Fig. 3.

Those in conflict can either engage in it or avoid it. Usually people default to one particular mode of conflict resolution. The style, however, might vary according to different contexts or relationships. It is important to note that our ability to address the many conflicts we face each

---

16 Used with permission from "Conflict and Negotiation Process in Organizations" by K. Thomas, 1992. In M. D. Dunnette and L. M. Hough (Eds.), *Handbook of Industrial and Organizational Psychology* (2nd ed., vol. 3, p. 660). Palo Alto, CA: Consulting Psychologists Press. Copyright 1992 by L. M. Hough. Adapted with permission.

day depends on how flexible and willing we are to match the appropriate conflict resolution style to the situation and the relationship. Each of the five modes of conflict resolution can be called upon, depending on the situation. William Wilmot and Joyce Hocker explain this well in their book, *Interpersonal Conflict*.[17] Avoidance, for example, is useful if an issue is trivial or not terribly important; avoidance can keep a relationship intact, can buy time, and can be used to defuse an emotional or volatile situation. The competitive style is characterized by aggressive and uncooperative behavior—pursuing our own concerns at the expense of another. People with competitive styles use direct confrontation, trying to prove they are right and win the argument.[18] Competition can be appropriate and useful when a quick and decisive action must be taken such as in an emergency. Also, in certain customer situations, a competitive style might be needed to bring customer satisfaction. Compromise is an intermediate style resulting in some gains and some losses for each disputant. Compromise requires trade-offs, and it sometimes lets disputants accomplish important goals with less time expenditure than collaboration requires. It can be used as a back-up method for decision making when other styles fail.[19]

Those who practice accommodation do not assert individual needs and prefer a cooperative and harmonizing approach. When we find that we are wrong, it can be best to accommodate the other to demonstrate reasonableness. Also, if an issue is more important to one party than to the other, it may be best to give a little in order to gain a lot. If harmony or maintenance of the relationship is currently the most crucial goal, accommodation allows the relationship to continue without

---

17 Wilmot and Hocker, 139–163.

18 Ibid., 145.

19 Ibid., 156–157.

overt conflict.[20] Collaboration demands the greatest degree of engagement of any of the conflict styles, and it can be the most time-consuming. "Collaboration shows a high level of concern for one's own goals, the goals of others, the successful solution of the problem, and the enhancement of the relationship."[21] "Collaboration generates new ideas, shows respect for the other party, and gains commitment to the solution from both parties."[22] In working with those in conflict, it is helpful if they bring some awareness to their usual (or default) style of conflict resolution and the modes they have used regarding the particular conflict we are discussing with them.

---

20 Ibid., 158–159.

21 Ibid., 161.

22 Ibid., 162.

Chapter Five

Consultant Qualifications

Do you need to be a qualified mediator to be a conflict resolution consultant?

The scope of both mediation and coaching has grown a great deal over the last twenty years. There are thousands of people who call themselves coaches or mediators, and many centers offer coaching or mediation services. None of these is regulated by a state license. Only a handful are regulated by a certification limited to the program. Even fewer are regulated by an accreditation of training programs method. Yet in most professions, quality assurance is obtained through a licensing or certification program. Conflict resolution consulting is complex. It involves the use of highly tuned skills, and is called for when people are at a vulnerable time in their lives. It is not coaching and it is not mediation; however, it is designed to follow the basic principles of mediation, and therefore consultants must first be trained as qualified mediators.

So what is the difference between conflict consulting and coaching? Why do conflict resolution consultants follow mediation principles and not coaching principles? Coactive coaching is defined by the

Coaches Training Institute[23] as "a powerful alliance designed to forward and enhance the lifelong process of human learning, effectiveness, and fulfillment." Mediation is broadly defined as "a dispute resolution method in which a neutral third party meets with the opposing sides to help them find a mutually satisfactory solution."[24] Based on these definitions, conflict resolution consulting is more like mediation for one party than it is like coaching. The key word in the coaching definition is "alliance"; the coach and participant work in partnership to move the participant forward in key areas. The key word in the mediation definition is "neutral"; the mediator does not form an alliance, is not a partner, and has no agenda to help move a person forward. The consultant, like the mediator, is neutral, impartial, and has no independent agenda other than to follow the lead of the participant and help the client come up with a conflict resolution plan.

Impartiality and Neutrality

There is a great deal of power in impartiality and neutrality. The simple fact that the consultant has no vested interest in the outcome of the situation that brought the party to conflict consulting, and that the agenda is to follow the participant's agenda, is what sets conflict resolution consulting apart from coaching. Your job is not to rely on your knowledge of who the particular person is, or his or her patterns, history, personality, or other factors that may contribute to the conflict.

"There is a great deal of power in impartiality and neutrality."

Your knowledge of the law, judicial precedent, family dynamics, or cultural issues are of no concern to you. You need to remain a blank slate; you are there to listen, summarize, reframe, acknowledge, support, and in some cases teach (upon request). To be impartial, you must appear impartial. This means the participant should not have met or spoken to you

---

23 www.thecoaches.com (Accessed February 2012).
24 http://legaldefinition.us/mediation.html (Accessed February 2012).

before, and you should not have met or spoken to the other disputant. Appearances make a difference. Striving for impartiality means that the consulting process is untainted by the consultant's biases and prejudices, so that the disputant can focus on resolving his or her own concerns, rather than have to respond to input from the consultant. The consultant creates a channel for communication and is not an obstacle to it, and remaining impartial allows for the channel to be as unimpeded as possible.

A joint undertaking by the American Arbitration Association (AAA), the American Bar Association (ABA), and the Society of Professionals in Dispute Resolution (SPIDR) produced the Model Standards of Conduct for Mediators, which defines "impartiality as evenhandedness and lack of prejudice based on the parties' personal characteristics, background or performance at the mediation."[25] In reality, it is very difficult to keep our individual biases and prejudices out of mediation or consulting sessions. Sometimes without being fully aware of this, we are sizing up people as soon as we meet them. We notice how they dress, their speech patterns, their pace, body language, race, hair type and color, facial characteristics, gender, class, education, and the like. We make assumptions based on these and other factors; we compare people to others we know, or to ourselves. We think about how we would handle a similar situation, or perhaps we are reminded of a similar situation we experienced.

The key to impartiality lies in our ability to recognize that we do have our own biases and perspectives, and we can self-manage so that they do not interfere with our effectiveness as a neutral consultant. If you feel uncomfortable with a person, have trouble making eye contact, or feel judgmental or impatient, you may be bumping up against some challenges to impartiality. If this occurs, try to bring yourself back to your commitment to empowering people to resolve their own conflicts.

---

25 *ADR Bulletin*, Vol. 5, No. 3, 2002, Art. 7.

You are not there to judge, to solve the problem, or to demonstrate your brilliance. You are there to help the person discover their own inner brilliance and ability to create lasting solutions to problems.

Offering Advice

In the facilitative model, mediators do not give advice, recommendations, or come up with ideas. The facilitative mediator asks questions, validates and normalizes parties' points of view, searches for interests underneath the positions taken by parties, and assists the parties in finding and analyzing options for resolution. A mediator using this style is completely neutral. He or she does not give advice, recommendations, or opinions. The mediator serves as a channel of communication and is focused on ensuring a continued dialogue. Through questioning, validating, searching for underlying interests, and analyzing, the mediator structures the process. The parties are in charge of the outcome. Conflict resolution consulting can be described almost identically: the consultant asks open-ended questions, validates and normalizes the participant's point of view, searches for interests underneath the positions taken by the participant, and assists the participant in finding and analyzing options for resolution. A consultant is completely neutral. He or she does not give advice, recommendations, or opinions.

The conflict consultant serves as a channel of communication and is focused on ensuring a continued dialogue. Through questioning, validating, searching for underlying interests, and analyzing, the consultant structures the process. No recommendations are made and no opinions or solutions are given to the participant. The participant is in charge of the outcome of the consulting session.

Recognizing Directive Impulses

Mediation is designed to empower participants to arrive at their own resolution, and conflict resolution consulting is no different. However, it may be more difficult for some conflict consultants to curb their directive impulses, because there is no second party present to perceive that the direction provided is slanted toward one party or the other. During a conflict resolution consulting session, the participant might be feeling hopeless or stuck; it would be very easy for the consultant to make a suggestion, point them in a particular direction, or come up with an idea. Perhaps one of the most powerful features of a conflict consulting session is the validation provided to the participant that they have all that it takes to resolve the situation. When an idea belongs to the consultant and not to the party, it does not elevate the confidence of the party or affirm that the party has the tools to create a conflict action plan. Just as a mediation session belongs to the parties, the conflict consulting session belongs to the one participant.

The model of conflict resolution consulting promoted in this handbook asks the consultant to make every effort not to influence the person or impose an agenda. If you are thinking any of the following while you listen to a party, you are probably being directive in your communication:

> *How do I get them to…?*
> *That's not right, I can't let them…*
> *Maybe you're saying these things because…*
> *What's really bothering you is…*
> *This is getting nowhere…*
> *I know what you should do…*
> *What you're saying isn't helping…*

Also, if you find yourself saying any of the following out loud, you are probably exerting more influence and direction than is necessary to provide an empowering conflict consulting session:

Why don't you…
Have you tried this?
I have an idea; how about…
Wouldn't it be best if you…

Nondirective Communication

While it is impossible not to influence another, being nondirective means that your influence keeps decision-making and control with the party. *How does one accomplish this?*

- Listen actively using the guides to effective listening described in Chapter Eleven.
- Ask open-ended questions that show involvement and genuine curiosity for the party and that person's story.
- Let the party direct the conversation.
- Present options as they present themselves in the party's conversation.
- Check in with the party to assess whether the person is ready to make decisions.

A recent consulting case demonstrates the choices a consultant has in using nondirective communication. The consultant had a background as a tenant's rights attorney. The participant was an unhappy tenant considering terminating his tenancy due to several issues, both nonlegal and legal. The consultant, in listening to the tenant's story, had a running internal dialogue with such thoughts as: "The landlord can't do that!" "The tenant isn't following the law with regard to the notice to vacate." "Why in the world would the tenant pay rent after all that? The rent should be escrowed…"

Instead of offering legal advice, steering the tenant toward staying put or terminating, or sharing knowledge about consequences of any action the tenant might take, the conflict consultant should be asking some of the following questions:

> *Have you sought legal advice? What did you learn about your rights/responsibilities?*
> *Based on that knowledge, what do you think you should do?*
> *How will you go about doing that?*
> *What words would you use in the letter to the landlord?*
> *What do you want to do to resolve this?*
> *What are the steps you will take to make this happen?*

These sorts of questions put the participant in the driver's seat. Before the consulting session, the participant felt confused and in crisis. The session helped the tenant to see how much he had already done to resolve things with the landlord and to make decisions, and reinforced the tenant's plan and provided some structure for it. The tenant left the session feeling confident, more hopeful, and clear about next steps and the plan for the future.

Confidentiality

Confidentiality in conflict resolution consulting is important to encourage the participant to speak truthfully and candidly, to enable a full exploration of issues in dispute, and to set the stage for a satisfactory resolution. Conflict consultants have the privilege of being welcomed into a difficult moment in a person's life. Trust needs to be established quickly and privacy must be respected in order to assure an effective outcome. Confidentiality includes what you say to others, what notes

> "Conflict consultants have the privilege of being welcomed into a difficult moment in a person's life."

you keep, and who has access to them. Hopefully one outcome of a consulting session will be the successful scheduling of a mediation session between the disputants. If either party has had a conflict resolution consulting session, it is vital that the conflict consultant(s) do not later serve as mediators in the subsequent mediation session. It is important to disclose to the parties at the beginning of the mediation session if one or both of the parties participated in their own conflict resolution consulting session, and that nothing from that session can or will be disclosed during mediation. Also, inform the participants that the current mediators did not participate in conflict consulting with either party.

If the consulting participant has a conflict resolution action plan written up during the session, it is important to make clear that the action plan will not be disclosed to anyone, and cannot be subpoenaed by a court of law. Conflict consulting plans can be considered pre-mediation documents and should be covered by mediation confidentiality statutes. Of course, the participant is free to show a written conflict resolution plan to anyone he or she chooses. If the action plan is shown to the other disputant and the conflict ends up as a court case, it is possible to argue that the conflict action plan is a pre-mediation document and should be considered confidential and inadmissible in a court.

Conflict Resolution Consultant Liability

Conflict resolution consultants are mediators with additional specialized training. They may be governed by the same ethical rules and standards as mediators, and may enjoy the same immunity from lawsuits or other protections as may be enumerated in state statutes. Legislation in certain jurisdictions protects mediators from civil liability. Many states in the U.S. have statutes that provide some form of mediator immunity. If mediators/conflict consultants worry about being sued for making an error, they become rigid and lose creativity. Also, in facilitative mediation, as in conflict resolution consulting, what the mediators/consultants say or do is less important than what the participant says or does. A consultant is neutral, and is not there to influence the outcome of the issue at hand. The fact that the consultant is not responsible for resolving the conflict is the very reason they should not be liable for any actions or errors during a conflict consulting session. Immunity of conflict consultants allows for necessary encouragement for good-hearted people helpers to offer the vital service of conflict resolution consulting. The participant is assumed to have freely come to the session and to be open to exploring avenues of conflict resolution. It would be counterproductive to fail to extend mediator immunity to such consultants.

Barriers to Conflict Consulting

Martha came to the Conflict Resolution Center (CRC) with a litany of complaints against neighbors, former boyfriends, lawyers, and businesses. She was one of the first CRC conflict resolution consulting participants, and one of CRC's newly trained consultants was eager to be assigned to this case. After two exhausting hours of listening to Martha rant and vent about the injustice of just about everyone, the consultant ended the session wondering if he had really done Martha any good at all. Martha constantly asked the consultant for legal advice and did not seem receptive to redirection by the consultant. The consultant began to wonder if mental health issues were a barrier to Martha's being able to fully comprehend the limitations of a consulting session. Although Martha signed the agreement to participate in a session and received the information packet that explained what to expect, as well as the participant's role in the session, it seemed to the consultant that Martha was using the two-hour session to spill out every possible emotion and roadblock to resolution (short of multiple lawsuits with questionable legal bases).

In a different situation, Sarah showed up for mediation at CRC and was disappointed that Joe did not show up, even though he said he would. The co-mediators, who were trained as conflict resolution consultants, offered to use the two-hour time slot as a conflict consulting session. Sarah eagerly accepted. The co-conflict resolution consultants felt the session was productive but worried whether Sarah's mental health issues stood in the way of a satisfactory resolution. Similar to Martha's conflict consulting session, the consultants provided Sarah with contact information for many resources, including mental health services, debt counseling, and emergency assistance. The consultants wondered whether CRC staff should screen out participants with limited capacity due to mental health or other concerns. Interestingly, halfway into the conflict resolution consulting session, Joe showed up. CRC staff asked him if he would like to come back at a later time for a mediation session and he agreed. A week later, a new mediation session was set up with a new set of mediators, and this time, Sarah did not show up for the mediation. Joe, in turn, was given the option of using the time for conflict consulting and while there were some mental health and capacity issues facing Joe, the consultants helped him decide his next steps. The following week, a new mediation session was scheduled with a new set of co-mediators, and both parties actually showed up and reached an amicable agreement in less than two hours.

Should limited capacity be a barrier to conducting an effective conflict consulting session? In short, no. Conflict resolution consulting is an empowering process that takes people as they are. Diagnosis, capacity determination, and exclusion are not necessary. Even a person with very limited capacity can benefit from being listened to, feeling heard, and being encouraged to come up with a plan that works for that person. With effective reality testing and by providing of a list of resources for services outside of what a consultant can do, a plan can be created. In Martha's case, while the consultant felt overwhelmed and perhaps disappointed that no written plan came out of the session, Martha showed one hundred percent satisfaction in her session evaluation. The consultant was very effective in following Martha's lead. She wanted to use her time to tell her story and to express emotion. No one told her what to do or how to behave. No one judged her or treated her differently than any other human being. Her concerns were validated. With regard to Sarah and Joe, conflict consulting was exactly what they each needed to position them to later meet face to face and come up with a written resolution. They each walked out of CRC feeling validated, connected to community resources, and optimistic about a renewed relationship.

All adults are presumed to have capacity until they demonstrably prove otherwise. Only a court of law has the legal jurisdiction to determine the lack of capacity and incompetence.

Senior citizens, people with serious and persistent mental illness, youth, "quirky" people, people who make a full-time job out of filing lawsuits, are all invited to participate in conflict resolution consulting sessions. For example, an elder's personality traits sometimes become more pronounced with age. A proud person used to acting and being treated as an adult cannot imagine much less tolerate being told that he will now take orders from his children, and will resist doing so. This might make a person seem less rational or reasonable, but that doesn't justify devaluing the ability to function well in a conflict resolution consultation or family mediation setting. All adults have the right to be autonomous and act to preserve personal autonomy. That is, we have the right to make decisions and govern own lives, even when we appear to be unwise or irrational. Frailty, eccentricity, and vulnerability do not make a person incapable or without capacity to make personal decisions.

Chapter Six

Overview of the Stages of Conflict Resolution Consulting

As stated earlier, conflict consulting is a systematic, three-level model, providing an opportunity for disputants to express themselves and develop strategies on how to constructively move forward toward resolving their dispute when the other party has not yet come to the table. Conflict consulting can be broken down into three components: emotional expression, tactics/ skills, and action plan.

> "Conflict consulting can be broken down into three components: emotional expression, tactics/ skills, and action plan."

Emotional Expression: Allowing the party to vent about feelings and experiences is a very important aspect of the conflict consulting session. Emotional expression about the conflict provides a disputant with a sense of empowerment and is an opportunity for the participant to more objectively reflect on the situation. In venting emotions, the participant also clarifies and better understands some of the underlying issues of the conflict.

Tactics/Skills: During a conflict consulting session, the participant will learn new tools and skills that can be used both with the absent party and in other conflicts. A consultant can use the conflict resolution consulting session to rehearse communication with the other party, to prepare the party for mediation, and to coach the party in successful communication skills for use in any action plans formed during the session.

Action Plan: While the cancellation of a mediation session does prevent an agreement between the two parties, a mediator/consultant can help the participant try to move forward during the conflict resolution consulting session. Some ideas for discussion include developing strategies, brainstorming solutions, and using tools such as reality testing and conflict mapping. The mediator/consultant can also use the consulting session to provide the participant with referrals, and of course, discuss with the participant ways to encourage the other party to come to a mediation session.

Introductions/Opening

As in mediation, the opening stage of the conflict resolution consulting session is important for setting the tone of the mediation and making sure that the participant is comfortable and informed about the process

Storytelling

Following the consultant's opening remarks, it is important to provide the opportunity for the participant to talk as long as is needed to and tell the story.

Skills Building

After the emotional expression/storytelling phase, it may be appropriate to summarize what you have heard, state what issues the participant has raised, and possibly reframe as appropriate. You can move seamlessly into the skill-building phase by asking the participant what he or she might like to do to resolve this matter. You can offer some of the following teaching opportunities or possibly move right into them if the participant seems open to this. Some of the skills might include:

- Conflict mapping
- Role playing and reverse role playing
- "I" message instruction and coaching
- Conflict resolution style assessment
- Perspectives discussion

Conflict Resolution Action Plan

During the final phase of the session, the consultant clarifies with the participant what strategies they want to develop to address the conflict. The consultant may have the participant brainstorm possible solutions. The consultant can do reality testing and help the participant determine if the action steps are feasible. During this phase, the consultant can write up the action plan and provide the participant with a packet of written resources that might be utilized in moving toward resolution.

Closure

The session wrap-up is just as important as the opening stage. This is an excellent time to summarize what the participant accomplished in the session. Acknowledge the hard work. Affirm the skills the participant has, and remind the person about new skills learned. Ask about follow-up sessions and a plan to make sure the steps outlined in the action plan will be taken.

Chapter Seven

Opening the Session

As in mediation, the opening stage of the consulting session is important for setting the tone of the mediation and making sure that the participant is comfortable and informed about the process. Try to keep the opening statement short, while still covering the key points, and setting the participant at ease as much as possible. The Conflict Resolution Center provides the participant three forms before and/or during the session. These are:

1. Preparing for Your Conflict Consulting Session
2. Agreement to Participate in Conflict Consulting
3. Conflict Consulting Questionnaire.

The forms are reproduced on the following pages and cover information you will want to include in preparing a participant for conflict resolution consulting.

CONFLICT **RESOLUTION** CENTER
Helping find common ground since 1983

<u>**PREPARING FOR CONFLICT CONSULTING**</u>
Please read this sheet prior to your consultation. This should help you prepare.

WHAT IS CONFLICT CONSULTING?
Conflict consulting provides participants with an opportunity to explore their perspectives about the situation while assisting participants in developing their own constructive strategies and action plans. Participants will be given the opportunity to further develop skills and consider tactics that may help them develop their own solution. The consultation takes place in a private and confidential setting and participants are encouraged to be honest and open in exploring possible solutions. Services are available to all who want them and we will not deny anyone our services because of inability to pay. Conflict consultation can be used in almost any dispute and can help the participant move toward a solution.

WHO ARE THE CONSULTANTS?
All conflict consultants are trained and experienced in consultation and have completed conflict consulting training as well as mediation training under Minnesota Statutes 494.01 and 518.619. Our consultants come from a wide range of cultural, educational, and employment backgrounds. Consultants do not take sides, give advice or information, or tell you what to do. Consultants are impartial and neutral as they assist you in developing your own plan.

WHAT WILL HAPPEN AT THE CONSULTATION?
Consultation generally lasts about two hours. You can arrange more time or more sessions if necessary. The consultation starts with an opportunity to share what brought you to the consultation. You should be prepared to discuss what your needs and interests are in this conflict. This is an opportunity to lay out your concerns, not to "make your case." This is not a time for proving anything; it's about exploring possible solutions and understanding the nature of the conflict and what some possibilities might be for resolution.

The consultant may ask you some questions such as "What do you need?" "What do you want the other person to know?" The consultant will help you identify your most important needs. You will also be asked to consider the needs of the other person. It will be important to carefully consider the other person's understanding of the conflict, to develop an action plan that will be most likely to succeed.

After you have explored the perspectives, needs, and interests involved in the conflict, the consultant will assist you in identifying what skills and understanding may be helpful to develop before working toward a solution. The consultant may rehearse possible communications with the other person, prep you for mediation, or concentrate on successful communication skills for working toward resolution of the conflict. This process will also help you understand how you typically deal with conflict and consider the most productive ways to respond.

After a period of time in which you work on skills and understanding of conflict, you may choose to explore different options to resolve the issues at hand. There may be more than one issue to work on. Your consultant will help you to arrive at appropriate next steps. The consultant will not come up with the solutions for you nor make suggestions, provide ideas, or advice. You will make decisions that are right for you. You may think this is impossible, but you might be pleasantly surprised!

YOUR ROLE IN THE CONSULTATION
Consultation may not be a final solution to the conflict, but will help you develop carefully considered steps that can move it in the right direction. By identifying what the needs and issues are for you in this conflict, considering the other participant's concerns and needs, and exploring solutions to each issue that meet both parties' concerns, a plan for a lasting solution may be reached.

Fig. 4

CONFLICT **RESOLUTION** CENTER
Helping find common ground since 1983

Conflict Consultation Agreement

A conflict consultation is an opportunity for an individual to examine his or her situation with a trained conflict consultant. The process will help increase the participant's understanding of the situation, develop additional skills, and explore possible solutions. The consultant is not an authority figure and works with the participant to come to his or her own conclusions.

Participants retain their legal rights to pursue this matter in any way they see fit. The process allows participants to develop their own solution. Any oral or written action plan that proceeds from this process will be decided upon by the participant. Information divulged in the consultation process will remain confidential, including meeting notes.

In this consultation, it is important to be aware of these guidelines:

1. Participant is encouraged to engage the process with honesty and a desire to work toward a solution.

2. All communications and documents made during this process are confidential. All written notes will be disposed of.

3. Minnesota statute §595.02, Subdivision 1(l), makes testimony regarding any communications and documents made or used in the course of, or because of, mediation inadmissible at subsequent legal or administrative proceedings. Staff, files, and consultants of CRC cannot be subpoenaed to testify on behalf of any party. CRC feels that conflict consulting falls within the protections of the mediation statute.

4. Evidence of child abuse and/or abuse of a vulnerable adult will be reported. Also, threats of serious bodily injury directed at an individual or the substantial likelihood that an individual's actions, or inactions, may lead to the serious bodily harm of another will be reported.

5. The consultant will not provide legal advice or information. Decisions made by participants could adversely affect their legal rights. They should consult with an attorney before enacting any solution if they are uncertain about their rights.

6. The conflict consultation process is voluntary and should continue only if the process is serving the needs of the participant. The participant or consultant reserves the right to conclude the process at any point.

I have read and understand the above information:

_____/_____/_____
Date

_____   _____
Participant   Participant

_____   _____
Consultant   Consultant

Fig. 5

Conflict Resolution Consulting Questionnaire

Please complete part one **before** your conflict consulting session and part two **after** the session.

Your Name: _____   Today's Date: _____

Part One (before the session):

1. **The conflict I am here to discuss is:**

   _____

   _____

2. **Up until now, I have done the following to resolve this conflict:**

   _____

   _____

Part Two (after the session):

1. On a scale of 1 to 5 (1 means disagree and 5 means agree) rate the following (circle):
   I feel confident about how I can handle this dispute   1 2 3 4 5
   I know what to do next to resolve the situation   1 2 3 4 5
   I feel hopeful about the situation   1 2 3 4 5
   I have a better understanding of what the other person's viewpoint might be   1 2 3 4 5

2. The most helpful thing the conflict consultant did was:

   _____

   _____

3. I wish the consultant would have done this:

   _____

   _____

4. This session did / did not (circle one) meet my expectations (please explain):

   _____

   _____

Fig. 6

Conflict Consulting Opening Statement Checklist

The consultant opening remarks should contain the following: welcome and words of encouragement, housekeeping logistics, an explanation of the purpose and process, the consultant's role, an explanation of confidentiality, and signing of the Agreement for Conflict Consulting.

Welcome and words of encouragement

Introduce yourself. Cover logistical information. Acknowledge the person's decision to take this step toward resolving conflict.

Purpose of Conflict Consulting

Explain that conflict consulting provides participants with an opportunity to explore their perspectives about the situation while assisting them in developing their own constructive strategies and action plans. Participants will be given the opportunity to further develop skills and consider tactics that may help them develop their own solution. This is a one-party option that will include some emotional expression, skills development, and creation of a conflict action plan.

Process

Explain that this is a voluntary process and that this session will last no more than two hours.

Consultant's Role

The consultant helps a person in conflict find what the next step in this particular conflict might be. The consultant will not make decisions or tell the participant what to do, nor will the consultant give legal advice or suggest how to resolve this issue. The consultant may offer to teach some skills and do some rehearsing about how to speak to the other party. The consultant will be very clear when moving into a teaching role and then when moving out of it.

Confidentiality

The consultant will keep confidential what happens in the session. Confidentiality exceptions, such as child abuse, credible threats of harm, and criminal acts will be noted. Because the conflict consulting sessions sometimes occur as preparation for mediation and can be seen as part of the mediation process, CRC asserts that anything that happens in consulting session mediation cannot be used in court.

Agreement for Conflict Consulting

Review and sign the agreement for conflict resolution consulting. Check/confirm whether the matter is before any court, or if there are any related arrests or Orders for Protection.

Always ask if there are any questions.

Chapter Eight

Storytelling and Expressing Emotion

Storytelling

Following the consultant's opening remarks, it is important to offer the participant an opportunity to talk as long as is needed to tell the person's story. It is in our nature to tell stories; they bring meaning to our lives and validate who we are and what we stand for. By listening to a person's story, consultants learn how people make sense of the world. By telling stories of events and by giving meaning to these events, people construct their own reality. People in conflict will tell conflict stories that help them make sense of the situation, the other person, and themselves. It is very possible that the participant has not felt that anyone has listened to his or her story about this conflict. Perhaps the story was dismissed or ignored and the person didn't feel validated, or felt frustrated or hopeless. During the storytelling phase, the consultant's role is to listen and perhaps to ask some questions. The consultant is listening for some specific things, such as:

- What specifically did the participant hear or experience that caused him or her to reach a particular conclusion or react in a certain way?
- How did the negative encounter, problem, or issue impact the participant?
- What assumptions or interpretations does the participant have about the other person's behavior or about whom the other person is?
- What strongly held beliefs or values does the participant have that may have intensified this conflict?
- What interests or needs does the participant have?

What is Narrative Mediation?

Narrative mediation emphasizes storytelling. The focus is on the stories individuals tell themselves, in that people live their lives according to stories that are socially and culturally construed. Narrative mediation focuses less on positions and interests as central to conflicts, and more upon how stories, which emerge from a person's social and cultural background, shape conflict. A mediator using this style helps people examine their stories in order to overcome the divisiveness of a conflict. "Working from a narrative perspective places the cultural world, and power relations within it, at the center of the process of mediation."[26] "Narrative mediation uses a technique called deconstruction. The mediator asks questions that invite the participants *out of* the conflict story and *into* learning how they have been caught in the web of the dispute. Taken-for-granted aspects of 'how things are' can be viewed from a new perspective. Deconstructive conversation loosens the authority of a dominant way of thinking and opens the door for different ways of thinking."[27] To learn more about narrative mediation, see *Practicing*

26 http://narrative-meMediation.crinfo.org (Accessed February 2012).
27 Ibid.

Narrative Mediation by John Winslade and Gerald Monk, which provides mediation practitioners with practical narrative approaches that can be applied to a wide variety of conflict resolution situations.

Storytelling is vital to the success of a conflict consulting session. It might be helpful to examine the origins of the story with the participant. What are some of the assumptions, values, beliefs, and events that contributed to the story? Is it possible for the participant to step away and detach from the story as if an outsider reading a book or watching a movie? What is missing from the story? Since the story being told involves conflict, is it possible that it omitted elements that could result in cooperation, mutual understanding, or compromise?

> "Storytelling is vital to the success of a conflict consulting session."

Understanding Emotions

According to Tricia Jones and Andrea Bodtker, "Emotion is the foundation of all conflict."[28] If emotional messages are not read properly or if they are masked (making decoding difficult), this can lead to inadvertent conflict between people. Threats to identity and power produce negative emotions (feelings of our needs not being met). We might feel unfairly attacked or misunderstood, or feel inadequate, demeaned, or inconsequential. How we deal with threats to identity depends on our emotional competency. Emotional competency is the ability to recognize and manage one's own and others' emotions, to motivate oneself and restrain impulses, and to handle interpersonal relationships effectively. Emotional competency involves the ability to see many perspectives, to be emotionally aware, and to be culturally sensitive.

It helps to understand a few things about emotions. First, emotion often creates a physiological response, i.e., how you "feel" when experi-

---

28 See "Mediating with Heart in Mind: Addressing Emotion in Mediation Practice," *Negotiation Journal*, 17:3, July 2001, 217–244, and "Conflict Education in a Special Needs Population," *Mediation Quarterly*, 17(2), Bodtker & Jones, 1999, 109–124.

encing an emotion. One may have a bodily reaction to emotion; this is the felt or biological aspect of emotion. A physiological response that affects one's ability to think clearly is called emotional flooding or emotional overload. One often feels unable to think clearly if overwhelmed with emotions such as anger or sadness. Another term worth noting is emotional contagion; this is a physiological response to another person's emotion (e.g., if someone else tells you a sad story and chokes up, it brings a tear to your eye). This is not to be confused with commiseration, empathy, or compassion. Being impacted by another person's emotions is part of the human experience. Emotional contagion involves a person mimicking the emotional behaviors of others and responding to a situation based on the experience and emotions of the others.

Secondly, there is a cognitive component: how you evaluate/appraise/make sense of the event that causes the emotional experience. Negative emotions arise from appraisals that are perceived as getting in the way of your goals. Once a situation occurs, thoughts (cognitions) about the situation usually come before the emotion. Thoughts tend to create our feelings. Our appraisal of the situation will determine whether our emotion is negative or positive. For example, if my bike is stolen, I might think, "This is horrible, I will never be able to get to work on time now, I have no other way to get there; I'll lose my job…." This appraisal of the situation will most likely lead to emotions of anger, fear, and sadness. If I think about the situation and say to myself, "I am so glad I was not on that bike when it was stolen. I am lucky to be here, even if my bike is gone," chances are, I will be left with emotions such as hope and gratitude. How a person manages a situation determines the type of emotion he or she experiences. If I manage the stolen bike situation by feeling stuck and unable to go anywhere, I will probably feel negative emotions. If I manage it by telling myself that "this is not the end of the world" and begin to look into alternate means of transportation, my emotions will be less negative.

The final component to emotion is behavioral. Once a situation occurs, how do emotions get expressed to others, consciously or unconsciously? This is impacted by cultural rules and falls into nonverbal and verbal categories. Emotions are verbally expressed in many ways. These might include direct statements of emotion such as "I am so happy!" or "I feel angry," or they might be statements that involve blaming another or one's self, or verbal outbursts. Volume and pace of speech might also vary depending on cultural norms and personality. Nonverbal behavior that indicates emotional expression might include personal affect, posture, silence, touch or lack of touch, and physical proximity.

Emotional Expression

It is essential that a participant be given ample time to express emotion while telling the story. It has long been recognized that inhibiting the expression of emotions has a negative impact on both physical and psychological health. Studies have shown that emotional repression is linked to higher reports of medical problems such as chronic pain, immune dysfunction, and psychiatric conditions. There are many myths about strong emotions. People claim that emotions are irrational, negative, and cannot be controlled, and will escalate if released. The common viewpoint is that emotions should be ignored and that they are not helpful in making decisions.

Those of us who train mediators tell our students, "If you are uncomfortable with displays of emotion, do not become a mediator!" Emotions are useful in guiding us in understanding the origin and nature of conflict. You cannot rid yourself of emotion any more than you can rid yourself of your thoughts. Emotions may be uncomfortable for some to experience, but there is no "negative" emotion. Acknowledgment of even uncomfortable emotions can be liberating. Emotions can be controlled; we control them every day and release them as it feels necessary, safe, and liberating to do so. When emotional expression is invited and truly heard, people often feel free of the emotion. Usually, release of emotions has a cleansing effect; only rarely does the release of emotion escalate the emotion. Some people do have difficulty with anger management, but this is not the norm. Even domestic violence perpetrators do not necessarily have an anger management problem. These perpetrators control their anger and emotion quite effectively at work and with others they are not related to.

If emotions are ignored in a conflict resolution consulting session, they will surface at another time and probably interfere with reaching a sustainable solution. Our feelings guide us to our needs and our interests. They are to be embraced. Conflict consultants are not therapists, nor are they to be seen as the supportive friend. On the other hand, in order to help a disputant find a path to peace, the consultant needs to encourage expression of emotions. The job of a conflict resolution consultant is to recognize both the verbal and nonverbal signs of strong feelings. Some people are not able to name their feelings.

As a consultant, you may also acknowledge and validate feelings, name what you hear or see. You might say, "You sound sad." Don't worry if you get it wrong! If the person disagrees and corrects you, that will further help the person identify the real feelings. You can certainly ask the participant: "How did that make you feel?" "How do you feel right now?" or "What do you imagine the other person feels about this situation?" One of these questions might open a path to discovery of what the participant really needs.

In sum, participants benefit from identifying, acknowledging, and talking about the feelings associated with the situation. If feelings aren't addressed directly, they will leak out in damaging ways. Also, unexpressed feelings make it difficult to listen. Recognizing our feelings is challenging. Feelings are more complex and nuanced than we usually imagine. What's more, feelings are very good at disguising themselves as emotions we are better able to handle; bundles of contradictory feelings masquerade as a single emotion. As we grow up, each of us develops a characteristic emotional footprint whose shape is determined by which feelings we believe are okay to have and express and which are not. Don't treat feelings as gospel. Negotiate with them. Feelings are formed in response to our thoughts. This means that the route to changing your feelings is through altering your thinking. By disentangling intent from impact, and exploring both parties' contributions, we alter our perception in a way that changes our emotions.

The "chart of feelings" below might be a good place to start in helping a participant recognize his or her feelings.

Words That Express Feelings

accepted	edgy	irritated	sexy
afraid	elated	jazzed	shaky
ambivalent	embarrassed	jealous	shy
annoyed	enthusiastic	joyful	silly
anxious	envious	lonely	strong
angry	excited	loving	tender
ashamed	fearful	needed	tense
astounded	foolish	neglected	terrified
bashful	frustrated	nervous	tight
bewildered	furious	passionate	tired
bitter	glum	peaceful	trapped
bored	good	pessimistic	ugly
brave	grateful	playful	uneasy
calm	guilty	pleased	uptight
confident	helpless	pressured	vulnerable
confused	high	protective	warm
defeated	hopeful	puzzled	weak
defensive	hostile	rejected	wonderful
detached	humiliated	relieved	worried
disappointed	hurt	resentful	eager
inhibited	restless	ecstatic	intense
sad	disgusted	intimidated	sensual
disturbed	inadequate	sentimental	

Fig. 7. © 2005 by Center for Nonviolent Communication, website: www.cnvc.org, email: cnvc@cnvc.org. http://www.cnvc.org/Training/needs-inventory (Accessed February 2012). Used with permission.

Feelings When Your Needs are Satisfied

Affectionate	Confident	Grateful	Peaceful
compassionate	empowered	appreciative	calm
friendly	open	moved	clear headed
loving	proud	thankful	comfortable
open hearted	safe	touched	centered
sympathetic	secure		content
tender		**Inspired**	equanimous
warm	**Excited**	Amazed	fulfilled
	amazed	Awed	mellow
Engaged	animated	wonder	quiet
absorbed	ardent		relaxed
alert	aroused	**Joyful**	relieved
curious	astonished	Amused	satisfied
engrossed	dazzled	Delighted	serene
enchanted	eager	Glad	still
entranced	energetic	happy	tranquil
fascinated	enthusiastic	jubilant	trusting
interested	giddy	pleased	
intrigued	invigorated	tickled	**Refreshed**
involved	lively		enlivened
spellbound	passionate	**Exhilarated**	rejuvenated
stimulated	surprised	blissful	renewed
	vibrant	ecstatic	rested
Hopeful		elated	restored
expectant		enthralled	revived
encouraged		exuberant	
optimistic		radiant	
		rapturous	
		thrilled	

Fig. 8. © 2005 by Center for Nonviolent Communication, website: www.cnvc.org, email: cnvc@cnvc.org. http://www.cnvc.org/Training/needs-inventory (Accessed February 2012). Used with permission.

Feelings When Your Needs Are Not Satisfied

Afraid	**Aversion**	**Disquiet**	**Fatigue**	**Tense**
apprehensive	animosity	agitated	beat	anxious
dread	appalled	alarmed	burnt out	cranky
foreboding	contempt	discombobulated	depleted	distressed
frightened	disgusted	disconcerted	exhausted	distraught
mistrustful	dislike	disturbed	lethargic	edgy
panicked	hate	perturbed	listless	fidgety
petrified	horrified	rattled	sleepy	frazzled
scared	hostile	restless	tired	irritable
suspicious	repulsed	shocked	weary	jittery
terrified		startled	worn out	nervous
wary	**Confused**	surprised		overwhelmed
worried		troubled	**Pain**	restless
	ambivalent	turbulent		stressed out
Annoyed	baffled	turmoil	agony	
	bewildered	uncomfortable	anguished	**Vulnerable**
aggravated	dazed	uneasy	bereaved	
dismayed	hesitant	unnerved	devastated	fragile
disgruntled	lost	unsettled	grief	guarded
displeased	mystified	upset	heartbroken	helpless
exasperated	perplexed		hurt	insecure
frustrated	puzzled	**Embarrassed**	lonely	leery
impatient	torn		miserable	reserved
irritated		ashamed	regretful	sensitive
irked	**Disconnected**	chagrined	remorseful	shaky
		flustered		
Angry	alienated	guilty	**Sad**	**Yearning**
	aloof	mortified		
enraged	apathetic	self-conscious	depressed	envious
furious	bored		dejected	jealous
incensed	cold		despair	longing
indignant	detached		despondent	nostalgic
irate	distant		disappointed	pining
livid	distracted		discouraged	wistful
outraged	indifferent		disheartened	
resentful	numb		forlorn	
	removed		gloomy	
	uninterested		heavy hearted	
	withdrawn		hopeless	
			melancholy	
			unhappy	
			wretched	

Fig. 9. © 2005 by Center for Nonviolent Communication, website: www.cnvc.org, email: cnvc@cnvc.org. http://www.cnvc.org/Training/needs-inventory (Accessed February 2012). Used with permission.

Core Concerns of Those in Conflict

Roger Fisher and Daniel Shapiro, in their book *Beyond Reason: Using Emotions as You Negotiate*, published by the Harvard Negotiation Project, posit that there are five core concerns that generate emotions. These core concerns are human wants that are important to almost everyone in most negotiations to resolve conflicts. The core concerns are appreciation, affiliation, autonomy, status, and role. "The power of the core concerns comes from the fact that they can be used as both a lens to understand the emotional experience of each party and as a lever to stimulate positive emotions in yourself and in others."[29]

The five concerns are not distinct from one another, but merge, each stimulating the emotions. Therefore, each concern must be met to the appropriate extent, which will be different in each negotiation. These concerns can be used to understand each party's emotional experience, as well to stimulate positive emotions in parties. Let's briefly look at each concern, emotions that arise from each concern, and what people tend to do once those emotions arise.

Appreciation

A person who is appreciated not only feels enthusiastic, affectionate, cheerful, and caring, but also tends to cooperate more. A person who is unappreciated will often feel angry and disgusted, often leading to reactions that are negative and contrary to desired interests. Fisher and Shapiro describe three main obstacles to achieving mutual appreciation: failing to understand another's point of view, criticizing the merit of another, and failing to properly communicate your own merit. To overcome these obstacles, one must first listen to words and recognize the emotional response of the other person; second, acknowledge the reasoning and beliefs behind the person's thoughts and feelings; third,

---

29 Roger Fisher and Daniel Shapiro, *Beyond Reason*. Penguin Books, 2005, 18. All materials used with permission.

disregard age, wealth, or authority; and finally, craft the message so others correctly understand.

Affiliation

Affiliation describes the sense of connectedness with another group or person. Treating people as colleagues results in their feeling more amused, compassionate, and ecstatic, which in turn tends to make them more amenable to collaborating. The person who is treated as an adversary is more apt to feel resentful or irritated. This person will be more prone to go it alone rather than work together. Often we fail to recognize the commonality between groups. Building affiliation bridges the gap between groups and increases the ability to productively work together.

> "The person who is treated as an adversary is more apt to feel resentful or irritated."

Autonomy

When a person's freedom to decide is acknowledged, emotions such as being proud, happy, and accomplished are evoked. These emotions tend to make a person prone to creativity. On the other hand, when autonomy is impinged, the emotions of guilt, shame, and remorse often arise, leading to more rigid thinking. The authors Fisher and Shapiro suggest using the Inform, Consent, and Negotiation system (I-C-N). A joint brainstorming session is an example of the inform step; it provides recommendations and options for mutual benefit. Consulting others before deciding, and negotiating for the best alternatives, ensures equality in representation. These steps help ensure the autonomy of each participating party.

Status

A person whose status is recognized will often feel more calm, relieved, and relaxed. This tends to make a person more prone to be trustworthy. Attacking a person's status causes humiliation and embarrassment. People with these feelings often are more prone to act deceptively and be seen as untrustworthy. (Note that they are seen as untrustworthy, but are not necessarily untrustworthy people.) "Status refers to our standing in comparison to the standing of others."[30] Positive emotions can result when status increases self-esteem or the influence over others. Negative emotions arise out of the competition for status. Acknowledging another's status before acknowledging your own can elicit positive emotions. This acknowledgment can be in a particular status, or the standing within a specific field, if the particular expertise can benefit the negotiation process. But status has its limits: the opinions of a person with a higher status are not automatically correct.

Role

When a person's role is fulfilling and includes activities that illustrate and convince the person that they make a difference, feelings of hope arise. Hopeful people often are more trustworthy, similar to the above description related to status. When people are trivialized and restricted, they may feel envious, jealous, or apathetic. As with status, these feelings cause behavior that appears to others as deceptive and untrustworthy. Remember that not all roles are permanent. Adopting temporary roles are helpful in fostering collaborations.

Addressing Strong Negative Emotions

Fisher and Shapiro stress that expressing strong emotion has several purposes:

- Gets emotions off your chest.
- Educates another about the impact of their behavior on you.

---

30 Ibid., 95.

- Influences the other person.
- Improve the relationship (clarification of intentions).

When strong emotions arise, attention narrows and thinking clearly is difficult. Fisher and Shapiro offer advice to resolve the tunnel vision created by negative emotions. They suggest observing differences in the other person's behavior and your own. When you feel things are heating up, find ways to soothe the situation (e.g., acknowledge concerns, take a break, or change the location of negotiations). Having a strategy to deal with negative emotions before entering into a negotiation is strongly advised. Fisher and Shapiro also suggest that you identify why strong negative emotions are being expressed, and evaluate the core concern that needs to be addressed.

By addressing and using the five core concerns to manage emotional response, relationships can be greatly improved. *Beyond Reason: Using Emotion as You Negotiate* transforms negotiation from an uncomfortable, unproductive process into an effective interaction of problem solving. The next several pages contains worksheets that conflict resolution consultants can present to participants to work through the conflict and to examine how core concerns and emotion may be a catalyst for conflict resolution. These materials were taken from "The Beyond Reason Preparation Guide," based on the ideas of *Beyond Reason: Using Emotions as You Negotiate.*[31]

- If your participant is concerned about emotional flooding when approaching the other party to discuss the conflict, coach the participant on how to deal with strong emotions.
- Ask about the participant's susceptibility to flooding.
- Identify "hot buttons." What triggers emotional flooding?
- Identify what can be done to calm down.

---

31 *Beyond Reason: Using Emotions as You Negotiate* (Viking, 2005) is reproduced with permission from Roger Fisher, Daniel L. Shapiro, Ph.D., and Zoe Segal-Reuchlin. For additional negotiation resources, visit www.beyond-reason.net.

- Take a break.
- Get some distance.
- Count to ten.
- Mindful/deep breathing.
- Stretch tense muscles.
- Visualization: imagine yourself in a calm, soothing place/ situation (go to your "happy" place).

A. My Conflict

Who are the parties:

What are the issues:

B. My Core Concerns

1. **Appreciation:** Do you feel misunderstood? Unheard? Devalued? Why?

2. **Affiliation:** Do you feel distanced? Excluded? Why?

3. **Autonomy:** Do you feel that your freedom to make choices is constrained? Why?

4. **Status:** Do you feel demeaned? Put down? Why?

5. **Role:** Do you feel unfulfilled in what you are doing? Why?

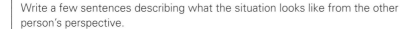

C. Step Into Their Shoes

Write a few sentences describing what the situation looks like from the other person's perspective.

"The way I see the situation ....

D. Anticipate Their Core Concerns

1. **Appreciation:** Do you (as the other person) feel misunderstood? Unheard? Devalued? Why?

2. **Affiliation:** Do you (as the other person) feel distanced? Excluded? Why?

3. **Autonomy:** Do you (as the other person) feel that your freedom to make choices is constrained? Why?

4. **Status:** Do you (as the other person) feel demeaned? Put down? Why?

5. **Role:** Do you (as the other person) feel unfulfilled in what you are doing? Why?

A. Stimulate Positive Emotions in the Other

1. Express Appreciation

- What questions can you ask to better **understand** and **find merit** in what the person thinks, feels, and has done?

- How might you **communicate** your enriched understanding?

2. Build Affiliation

- What **common interests** might you talk about?

- How will you establish yourselves as **joint problem solvers**?
  (e.g., "We are facing some tough challenges. How do you recommend we proceed?")

- What might you say or ask to **connect on a personal level**?
  (e.g., "My kids kept me up all night.")

3. Respect the Other's Autonomy

- What **process** might you suggest to structure the negotiation?

- What **habits** of yours might impinge upon the other's autonomy?
  (Do you talk too much? Listen too little?)

- How can you **check** this behavior?

4. Acknowledge the Person's Status

- In what ways does he or she hold high **social status**?

- In what areas of expertise or experience do they hold high **particular status**?

- How will you **communicate respect** for this status?
  (e.g., "You have more experience in...and I have more experience in...We can use this to our advantage.")

5. Enhance the Other's Role

- What roles might you play to foster collaboration?
  (e.g., problem solver, listener, evaluator)

- What might you do or say to help the person adopt a more fulfilling role?
  (e.g., *Problem solver:* "What's your advice on...."; *Option Generator:* "How about we take a couple minutes to brainstorm some options?"

B. Stimulate Positive Emotions in Yourself

1. Appreciation

- What are big points you want the other to understand?

- What stories or facts can you draw on to help the other appreciate your perspective?

2. Affiliation

- Remind yourself of something that makes you feel connected to the other, such as _____. (e.g., both have kids, both worked late last night, both have to report to a tough boss)

- Remind yourself of a positive relationship in your life, such as
  _____.

3. Autonomy

- Remember: You have more autonomy than you think.

- List some of the many choices you have the power to make:
  (e.g., to walk away; to commit; to take a break; to think what you want to think)

4. Status

- Remind yourself (and the other?) about a lofty status you hold, such as
  _____.

5. Role

- What activities can you incorporate into your role to make it more fulfilling?
  (e.g., work on listening for his or her interests; work on brainstorming creative options)

Used with permission from Roger Fisher, Daniel L. Shapiro, Ph.D., and Zoe Segal-Reuchlin. For additional negotiation resources, visit www.beyond-reason.net.

Chapter Nine

Helper's Tool Box

Asking the Right Questions

The way you ask questions, and the kinds of questions you ask, in conflict resolution consulting differ from those asked by life coaches, executive coaches, or conflict coaches. Coaches are trained to ask "powerful questions." These questions invite introspection, lead to greater creativity or insight, and invite participants to look inside or into the future. An example might be "Put yourself six months into the future; standing there, what decisions would you make today?"[32] This question gently guides the participant in a certain direction. This can be very powerful. However, this is not the kind of question a conflict resolution consultant is encouraged to ask. Consultant questions are short, open-ended, and based on things the participant has said, not ideas the coach has. These are some questions the consultant might ask to help the participant get to the heart of the matter:

---

32 From Coaches Training Institute, *Co-active Coaching Manual: New Skills for Coaching People Toward Success in Work and Life* by Laura Whitworth, Karen Kimsey-House, Henry Kimsey-House, and Philip Sandahl, Co-Active Space, 2000.

Questions to Get at Interests

1. Why is that important to you?
2. What matters to you most?
3. Say more about your basic concerns with this.
4. What is it that concerns you about this?
5. What leads you to say that?
6. Can you say more about how you see things regarding this?
7. What information might you have that would help them understand your concerns?
8. What specific information is in your mind about this? Are there any past experiences that influence how you're thinking about this?
9. What would help you feel better about this issue?
10. What would it mean to you if X happened?
11. How does your view about the intentions of your [neighbor/coworker/parent/etc.] make you feel?
12. What motivated you to take action X?

Questions to Address Feelings

1. Tell me what would help you feel better about that.
2. How do your assumptions/speculations/beliefs about this situation make you feel?
3. How does your view about your [neighbor's, coworker's, etc.] intentions make you feel?
4. What motivated you to take that action?
5. How might your actions have impacted your [neighbor, coworker, etc.]?
6. Is there anything that you've heard here today that changes your feelings about the situation?

7. Are there actions that either of you have taken that magnify the feelings, for better or worse?

8. It sounds like this is really important to you…tell me more about your feelings about that.

9. What leads you to say that?

10. How are you feeling about all of this?

11. Were you reacting to something that was said?

12. What impact did the actions have on you?

13. How do you see it differently?

14. Can you say more about why you think this situation was caused by your [neighbor, coworker, etc.]?

15. What would it mean to you if that happened?

Questions to Get Solutions and Test Reality

1. How would you want that handled if it happened again?

2. What ideas do you have for resolving this?

3. What could make this plan work for you?

4. How would we test that hypothesis?

5. What would it mean to you if that happened?

6. Is there anything that could be said that would persuade you to act/think differently?

7. Could you imagine a way of doing it differently that would not lead to the problem happening again?

8. What might happen if this idea were tried?

9. How might others [e.g., the neighbors, coworkers, etc.] view this?

10. How will you handle it if a problem comes up?

Questions that Get to the Heart of the Matter

1. What would it be like if you didn't have this friendship anymore?
2. Does it seem reasonable that there would be a labor charge?
3. What efforts have been made to resolve this problem?
4. What would "resolve it" mean to you?
5. Is there anything you'd like to do?
6. What does the money represent to you?
7. What does a compromise look like?

Positions vs. Interests

When working with a person in conflict, it is best to focus on needs and interests and not on positions. Getting at interests and needs is best accomplished by asking, "What do you need?" "What are you interested in?" An interest is not a solution. An interest is why you would like that outcome, or what you would like to avoid in order to reach an agreement. A need is what we must have to survive emotionally and physically. Needs include safety, belonging, achievement, autonomy, connection, health, well-being, etc. A position is a fixed proposal or solution that meets one's needs or interests. A position dictates what the other party must do—that the other party has to change, and the outcome is win/lose. You might consider asking the person to consider the following:

1. What are my goals/needs? What do I think the other person's goals/needs are?
2. What are the issues to be negotiated from my point of view? From the other person's point of view?
3. What common ground is there between us?
4. What do I need to know in order to understand the other's point of view?

5. What does the other need to know in order to understand my point of view?

6. What can I give him or her? What can he or she give me?

7. What are possible options for resolution?

Much of what a conflict resolution consultant does is to separate a participant's stated position from the underlying interests and needs, which are often more important in ensuring that the conflict is resolved. On top of this, the conflict often is resolved more easily when the consultant helps the participant resolve interests or needs rather than positions. Consider it a journey, starting with the parties' respective positions, advancing to a solution borne out of needs, as illustrated below.

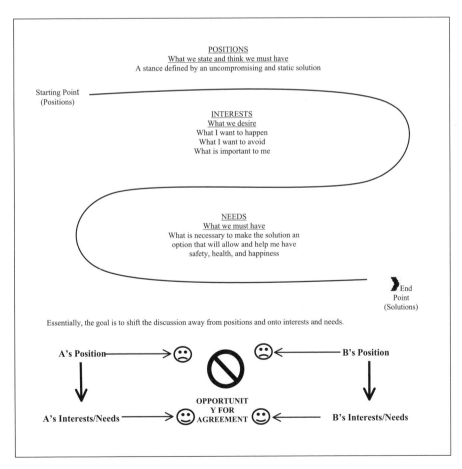

Fig. 10

Separate the People from the Problem

- Give each person a stake in the outcome by involving the person in the process.
- Allow each person to reconcile an agreement with the person's own principles and self-image.
- Listen actively and acknowledge what has been said.

Focus on Interests NOT Positions

- Look for basic human needs (security, economic well-being, sense of belonging, love, freedom).
- List all underlying interests.
- Be hard on the problem, but soft/flexible with the people.

Look for Mutual Interests and Concerns

- Create options without editing or analyzing.
- Avoid "either/or," "take it or leave it" statements.
- Look for shared needs, interests, and solutions offered.

Consulting About Having Difficult Conversations

In a consulting session, the participant may choose to speak directly to the person with whom there is conflict or invite that person to a mediation session. It is important to acknowledge that these kinds of conversations can be difficult. To prepare before going into a difficult conversation, you might ask the participant some questions:

1. What is your purpose for having the conversation? What do you hope to accomplish? What would be an ideal outcome?

Summarizing, Reframing and Other Skills

Skills	To Do This	<u>Examples</u>
Validate	• Directly acknowledge feelings/ issues. • Appreciate efforts/acts of parties.	1. So you're really bothered by...? 2. I appreciate you explaining your concerns.
Reflect	Say back to party what you believe was said, use language close to party's—use same substance and tone, don't parrot.	1. What I am hearing is...? 2. What you seem to be saying is...? 3. In other words...
Encourage	• Don't agree or disagree. • Use neutral language. • Use varying voice intonations.	1. I understand this is difficult, take your time. 2. I see this is really important to you.
Clarify	• Ask questions. • Restate wrong interpretations to force speakers to explain further.	1. Can you tell us more about...? 2. What did you mean by...? 3. What do you want Ms. Y to know on that?
Restate	• Restate basic ideas and facts. • Check to make sure you got it right.	1. So you would like a better relationship with your neighbors?
Summarize	• Restate major expressed ideas and feelings. • Condense what the speaker said into essential points.	1. So what you want to talk about today is... 2. Let me summarize what we've discussed so far. 3. So the concerns that have brought you to mediation are...?
Check In	• Ask parties whether a decision point you have noticed is one they want to consider and/or act upon. • Inquire whether they agree with your observations as to their dynamics.	1. What would you like to discuss next? 2. Are you comfortable with the way things are going so far? 3. Are you ready to move on to X? Do you want to stay with this point a bit longer? 4. Are you finding this discussion helpful?

Fig. 11. Reprinted with permission from Safe Horizon Mediation Center (Now New York Peace Institute), Basic Mediation Skills Handbook, 2009.

2. What assumptions are you making about this person's intentions? Be careful and remember—impact does not necessarily equal intent.

3. What "buttons" of yours are being pushed? Are you more emotional than the situation warrants?

4. How is your attitude toward the conversation influencing your perception of it?

5. How might their perspective differ from yours? What is it?

6. What are your needs and fears? Are there any common concerns? Could there be?

7. How have you contributed to the problem? How has the other person?

If the participant's purpose is to share, to understand, and to learn, a conversation might be warranted. If the purpose is to get the other person to admit he or she is wrong or to solve the short-term problem without addressing the underlying and long-term issues, a conversation might not be a good idea.

There are steps to a successful outcome, which include remembering to breathe, staying centered, and monitoring your emotions. The following steps can also be followed:

Step 1: Use a soft entry.

Step 2: Introduce the problem or challenge from your perspective. If this is difficult for you, say so. If not, don't.

Step 3: Cultivate an attitude of inquiry, discovery, and curiosity. Let the other person express his or her perspective—fully.

Step 4: Acknowledge this perspective.

Step 5: Problem Solving. If you are ready to begin building solutions, brainstorming and continued inquiry are useful; ask your opponent/partner what might work. Use something he or she said that you find agreeable enough to build on (reframing).

If the conversation becomes adversarial, go back to Step 3. Asking for the other's point of view usually creates safety, and they'll be more willing to engage.[33]

Teaching Attending Skills[34]

Having good attending skills means that we know how to listen. Using good attending skills means that we will have fewer difficult conversations. Most research supports the idea that 65–85 percent of what we communicate is nonverbal. If true, this means that what we do is often more important than what we say. These skills are necessary for the important talks, but they are vital to all good communication. Practice daily with people you like and are comfortable with, so that when you really need them, you'll be ready. Here are the basics:

Posture: Demonstrate relaxed alertness and involvement. Being relaxed shows that you accept the speaker and what the speaker is saying. Being alert shows that you are paying attention. This type of posture can include the following examples:

- Sitting forward or leaning into the speaker.
- Directly facing the speaker.
- Sitting physically open. Crossed arms and/or legs can communicate defensiveness and emotional distance.
- Use good personal space. Don't crowd the speaker. It often works to let him or her determine comfortable spacing. Americans prefer three feet or a little more than arm's distance.

---

33 Adapted in part from the work of Judy Ringer. "Making Difficult Conversations Easier," Spring 2008. This material has been created by Edmond Otis, MS, MFT, and Edmond Otis & Associates, Inc., for the Infopeople Project [infopeople.org], supported by the U.S. Institute of Museum and Library Services under the provisions of the Library Services and Technology Act, administered in California by the State Librarian.

34 Ibid.

- Don't fidget or sit like a rock. Your gestures, movements, and facial expressions should complement and be in response to the speaker's.

Eye Contact: This may be the most important component of good attending skills. Good eye contact communicates interest and confidence in the speaker's conversation. Eye contact, however, is cultural, and in some cultures it is unacceptable or even offensive to make eye contact.

- Look at the speaker, but don't stare.
- Allow for natural breaks.
- Allow people to avoid eye contact and initiate as they choose.

Find a Quiet Environment

- Find a quiet place with few distractions.
- Close the door.
- Turn off the TV, the phone, the radio, email, and the computer monitor (or at least make sure you can't see it); these are all natural distractors.

Difficult Conversations

The Harvard Negotiation Project teaches us that within each difficult conversation, there are three conversations. That is, there are three undercurrents driving the energy behind the conversation. The "what happened," the "feelings," and the "identity" conversations are all happening simultaneously.[35]

---

35 Sheila Heen, Douglas Stone, and Bruce Patton. *Difficult Conversations*. 2000.

The "What Happened" Conversation

This is the disparity between each party's interpretation of what has happened. Who is right? Who is to blame? We often get stuck thinking that our story is "right" and their story is "wrong," when in fact there is almost always some reasonable basis for each side's stories. We are in the habit of demonizing others' intentions and sanitizing our own: "If they did something that hurt me, it's because they meant to." "If I did something that hurt them, it was an unintended consequence—I had good intentions!" In this conversation, it is important to disentangle intent and impact. Just as it takes two to tango, most problems stem from things both sides said or did. With a few important exceptions, it is rarely helpful to assign blame for what went wrong. What is helpful is to explore what each side contributed to the problem. It is important to stress that in each conflict there are conflicting perceptions, interpretations, and values. Once disputants move away from the "truth" assumption and from the need to prove they are right, to understanding the differing perceptions of each side, reconciliation is possible. Once the participant shifts the focus away from establishing blame and toward an acknowledgment that we can never truly know another person's intentions, a conversation can lead to a stronger relationship.

> "It is rarely helpful to assign blame for what went wrong."

The "Feelings" Conversation

Despite our best efforts to conceal or deny our feelings, they tend to leak into conversations anyway. The problem is, they leak through in unproductive or even damaging ways. We question whether another person's feelings are valid. We argue with another person's feelings instead of acknowledging and validating them. Regardless of how much we try to check our emotions at the door, there are emotional undercurrents to most difficult conversations. Even more, difficult situations don't just *involve* feelings, they are *based on* feelings. Sometimes a situation is so sensitive that feelings can't even be broached. Typically, you will benefit from knowing how to acknowledge and talk about the feelings associated with the situation. The most effective way to move forward in a difficult conversation is to identify, acknowledge, and even discuss your feelings (and their feelings). The feelings conversation helps to unravel the complexity of emotions and defray the negative effects of leaking emotions.

The "Identity" Conversation

Conversations are difficult because they often threaten some part of our identity. For example, we might see ourselves as competent, generous, or fair, so anything that challenges that notion of ourselves knocks us off balance. It is important to recognize what's at stake in terms of identity in many difficult conversations. It is helpful when parties to a difficult conversation examine what the situation and the words spoken mean in terms of each person's self-image. There are judgments each person is likely making about the other. Such judgments affect self-esteem. Conflicting parties who suspend judgment about one another are better positioned to find resolution. The "Identity" conversation is often the most subtle and complex. However, it offers leverage in managing anxiety and improving results in the other two conversations. This conversation asks, "What does this say about me?" Even when you are the one who is delivering the bad news, identity still comes into play. People wonder how they will be seen after this conversation.[36]

In difficult conversations, we are encouraged to view the dispute through what is called the "Third Story." This means accepting that we think the *other person* is the problem and they think *we* are the problem! What's often hard to see is that what the other person is saying also makes sense. Each of our perspectives is valid for each of us because:

---

36 Ibid.

- Different information is available to each of us.
- We have different life experiences.
- We have different beliefs and values.
- We interpret things differently.
- We apply different implicit rules.
- Our conclusions reflect self-interest.

In difficult conversations, we are encouraged to accept that the other person's story is valid for that person, and to start from the third story, the story that encompasses perspectives from both sides. We are also encouraged to take these actions:

Disentangle impact from intention. We often incorrectly impute others' intentions based on the impact their actions have on us. Instead, it makes sense to examine 1) actions: what did the other person actually say or do? 2) impact: what was the impact of this action on me? and 3) assumption: based on this impact, what assumption am I making about what the other person intended?

Move from blame to mutual contribution. While the contribution may not be equal, it always takes two to tango. Blame creates defensiveness, limits learning, and hinders problem solving. Contribution is empowering. We may not be able to change the other person, but we can always change our part.

Prepare

Walk through the three conversations and core concerns before beginning the conversation.

Where to Start

Start from the third story. Describe what happened in a way that includes the other side. For example, "I've noticed a recurring argument we seem to have, where I see things this way and you see them that way. I'd like to talk about why that happens." It's almost never a question of right or wrong, so don't accuse the person; instead, invite the person to have a conversation with you.

Learning

Listen first to understand, then to be understood. You almost never know everything you need to know about the situation. Seek out the pieces of the puzzle you don't have.

Expression

You are an unparalleled expert on you. So, speak for yourself and how you are experiencing the problem. Don't speak for the person or assume you know what the other person is thinking or feeling.

Problem Solving

Take the lead. Be persistent about listening—mirror their words, paraphrase, ask for more information. Reframe their statements to distill the substance and emotion you hear. Name the troublesome dynamic in the conversation as it happens. Suggest more productive ways of talking to each other (e.g., "It might be helpful if we both agree not to call each other names"). Shift into problem-solving mode together (don't impose it on them), after you have learned as much as you can about their story.[37]

Does Blaming or Shaming Ever Work?

Many of us, at one time or another, blame or shame others as a way to express ourselves or resolve a disagreement; for some, blame and shame

---

37 Ibid.

are frequently used. How often do we hear someone say "You made me angry"? When we blame, we accuse another person of causing our experience. Shaming is an attack on a person's worthiness; it involves judging, criticizing, or insulting someone else. Blaming and shaming are attempts to project our bad feelings onto others. We may believe that if we can shift our pain onto another person, then we won't have to feel it. If we believe others are the source of our pain, then we can justify transferring it back to them. When a person blames or shames someone else, it causes the other person to feel both hurt and controlled. Blame and shame are so deeply embedded in our societal norms, and into common ways of communicating, that it may take some work to examine why we use these methods and what we need to do to find more effective ways of communicating. Firstly, blaming and shaming allow us to feel a sense of control, at least temporarily; it feels good to be "right." By using blame and shame, we manipulate others into doing what we want them to do. Shame may be used to deny our own responsibility and to place it elsewhere.

There are two ways people regularly defend themselves against failure. One way is by performing well for the reassuring admiration of others through wisdom, knowledge, status, money, or decent character, which may earn them the security of personal worth. Another way is resisting evidence of weakness by assigning blame to others.

Most of the data on assigning blame in relationships is based on research of domestic violence between couples. Very often, the abuser blames the victim for initiating the distress and even causing the abusive conduct. However, Dr. Scott of the University of Toronto and Dr. Strauss of the University of New Hampshire found that the dynamic of blaming may not be any different for ordinary feuding couples. "An individual who blames his partner for beginning arguments may also be highly likely to assign blame for the actions he or she takes during the argument."

"Why do you always start these fights?" "If you hadn't done that, we would have been better off." "Don't ask me now. You are the one who got us into this mess." "I didn't have anything to do with this." These are examples of statements that are likely to create shame, pain, and inadequacy for a partner. The hurt partner will withdraw from the other for safety and self-preservation.

Blaming and shaming are destructive communication tools that defeat the parties and cause harm. They are harsh tools used to establish superiority over someone else and damage the emotional safety of the party being blamed or shamed. Blaming serves only to shame and devastate the other person and seriously damages the relationship. When working with people in conflict, it is human nature to find a person to blame. The inclination will be to shame them until they fully acknowledge their responsibility for causing the problem. Your job as a conflict consultant will be to provide them with an alternative to the blame/shame game.

Chapter Ten

Conflict Mapping with the Participant

An effective conflict consulting tool is to "map" the conflict with the participant. A conflict map is a visual technique for showing the relationships between parties in the conflict. It was originally developed by Paul Wehr.[38] The conflict map helps parties reach a better understanding of the situation, to see more clearly the relationships between the parties and how power is distributed between them, to check the balance of one's own and the other's engagement, and identify entry points for action.

Conflict mapping may help people learn about their different viewpoints and perceptions. Paul Wehr, who developed a "Conflict Mapping Guide," asserts that the conflict map should include the following information:[39]

---

38 Paul Wehr. *Conflict Regulation*. Boulder, CO: Westview, 1979.

39 Adapted from Paul Wehr, Conflict Mapping, in: Burgess, Guy/Burgess, Heidi (eds.), *Beyond Intractability*, Conflict Research Consortium, University of Colorado, Boulder. Posted: September 2006 http://www.beyondintractability.org/essay/conflict_mapping/ (Accessed June 2011) and http://spot.colorado.edu/~wehr/40GD1.HTM (Accessed 23 June 2009). All materials used with permission. See also Wilmot and Hocker, 2001.

- Conflict history: What were the origins and major events in the evolution of the conflict and the context in which the conflict is situated?

- Conflict context: The scope and character of the context or setting within which the conflict takes place has to be established. Such dimensions can be geographical boundaries, relationships, communication networks and patterns, and decision-making methods.

- Conflict parties: These are the decisional units directly or indirectly involved in the conflict and having some significant stake in its outcome. Wehr distinguishes three kinds of parties:
  - *Primary parties*: These are individuals who oppose one another (whose goals are or are perceived to be incompatible). Often they are using fighting behavior. Primary parties have a direct stake in the outcome. The primary parties interact directly in pursuit of their goals
  - *Secondary parties*: They have an indirect stake in the outcome. Often, they are allies of sympathizers with primary parties, but are not direct adversaries.
  - *Third parties*: These are actors such as mediators and peacekeeping forces who might intervene to facilitate resolution. They have an interest in the successful resolution of the conflict.

Goals and interests: Wehr highlights that goals and interests are not the same. While goals are the more or less acknowledged objectives of parties in conflict and are usually expressed, interests are what really motivates the parties, what they really need to achieve: security, recognition, respect, etc.

Issues: A conflict will normally develop around one or more issues. Issues are points of disagreement and are often generated by one—or several—of the factors below:

- Facts-based: disagreement over what is, because of how parties perceive what is. Judgment and perception are the primary conflict generators here.
- Values-based: disagreement over what should be.
- Interests-based: disagreement over who will get what in the distribution of scarce resources, such as power, privilege, economic benefits, respect.
- Nonrealistic: originating elsewhere than in disparate perceptions, interests, or values.

Causes and consequences: It is not always possible to distinguish a cause of conflict from a consequence. As conflict emerges, cause and consequence tend to blend. Hostility might be a consequence of one phase of the conflict and a cause for the next.

Dynamics: A conflict is constantly moving and changing. Some dynamics could be these:

Polarization: As parties seek internal consistency and coalitions with allies, and leaders consolidate positions, parties in conflict tend toward bipolarization, which can lead both to greater conflict intensity or simplification making resolution easier.

Spiraling: Through a process of reciprocal causation, each party may try to increase the hostility or damage to opponents in each round, with a corresponding increase from the latter. De-escalatory spirals are also possible.

Conflict regulation potential: Each conflict contains its own conflict-limiting elements and this is where peace-building engagement could find entry points:

Internal limiting factors: values and interest the conflicting parties have in common, cross-pressures of multiple commitments of parties that constrain the conflict, etc.

External limiting factors: for instance a higher authority who could intervene and force a settlement or an intermediary from outside the conflict.

Interested or neutral third parties: These are trusted by all parties and could therefore facilitate communication, mediate the dispute, or locate financial resources to alleviate a scarcity problem.

Techniques of conflict management: Methods such as mediation, conciliation, rumor control, etc.

Considerations

1. Ask what the participant wants to map, when, and from what perspective. Ask then to choose a particular moment in a specific situation. In order to be helpful, the scope of your mapping exercise should not be too broad. It is often useful to do several maps of the same situation from different viewpoints. You can ask the participant how the different parties could see the very same situation differently. When mapping you can ask these questions:
   - Who are the main parties of this conflict?
   - What other parties are involved or connected in some way, including marginalized groups and external parties?
   - What are the relationships between all these parties? Try to present these on the map (alliances, close contacts, broken relationship, confrontation).
   - What are the key issues between the parties?

2. Have the participant place himself or herself in the map. Remind the participant that he or she is part of the situation and not external, even as it is being analyzed. Ask the participant how he or she might be perceived by others.

3. The mapping reflects a particular point in a changing situation and it points to action. This kind of analysis should be geared toward creating new possibilities. Therefore, use the mapping and ask the participant questions, such as: What can be done? Who can best do it? When would be the best moment? What is needed before and what should be done after?

4. It is also important to map the issues between the parties in conflict. Why does the conflict exist? What is the incompatibility? Also think about the position of the conflicting parties. What are their views of the groups involved in the situation?

The next several pages have examples of different kinds of conflict maps. It is not necessary to follow a rigid format. These forms can be modified or you can design your own form on the spot.

Conflict Map 1

Parties	What Happened	Feelings	Impact/Intent	Contribution
Who is Involved?	Party One's perspective	Party One's Feelings	Party One's Intentions	Party One's Contribution
	Party Two's perspective	Party Two's Feelings?	Impact of Party Two's actions on Party One	Party Two's Contribution
			Party Two's Intentions	
			Impact of Party One's actions on Party Two	
	*Discuss the fact that two people can see things differently based on the available information, life experience, and interpretation. The different perspectives are neither right nor wrong, but different. Use the **Perspective Pictures** to illustrate this point.*	*Discuss the role that emotions play in conflict. Give the party the **Feelings List** and ask him or her to circle all of the feelings that this situation has evoked.*	*Explain that we assume, often incorrectly, others' intentions from their impact on us. Actions: What did the other person actually say or do? Impact: What was the impact of this action on me? Assumption: Based on this impact, what assumption am I making about what the other person Intended?*	*Discuss the fact that blame leads to judging, while contribution leads to understanding. Understanding is necessary to resolve the conflict.*

Conflict Map 1 (continued)

Underlying Needs	Needs and Solutions	Brainstorming	Action Steps
Party One's Underlying Needs	What Party One needs to resolve the issue	What are some possible solutions?	What steps will Party One take following the consultation?
Party Two's Underlying Needs	What Party Two needs to resolve the issue		
*Use **Maslow's Hierarchy of Needs Pyramid** to explain basic human needs. Then use the **Identifying Needs Worksheet** to practice.*		*Explain brainstorming and try it out here.*	*Practice any of the steps that can be practiced by role playing, using the **I Statements Worksheet**, etc.*

Fig. 12

Conflict Map 2

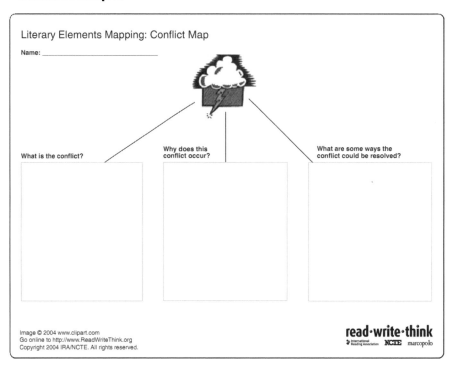

Fig. 13. Used with permission.

Conflict Map 3

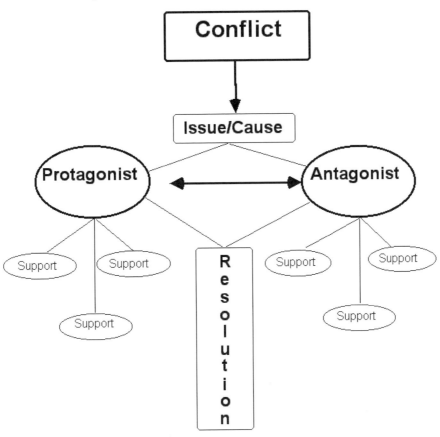

Fig. 14. Printed with permission from The Alliance for the Study and Teaching of Adolescent Literature at Rhode Island College. http://www.ric.edu/astal/litstrategies/mappingstrategies.html

Chapter Eleven

Skills Development

As mentioned earlier, conflict resolution consulting is arranged in three stages. Following the storytelling phase, it is possible to move into a teaching phase. It is not necessary to say, "Now we are going to move into a teaching phase." Usually the transition happens quite naturally. You might offer a transitional statement such as: "Would it be helpful to map out this issue?" or "What would Joe say about this situation if he were here, and how would you respond?" or "What would you like Joe to truly hear from you? What would your exact words be?" These transitional statements might lead you to move into conflict mapping, role playing, and/or learning about "I" message statements. However, you do not always need a skills building or teaching part of your conflict consultation. Some people come to the session equipped with everything they need and simply want your help putting their ideas into a concrete written plan. Others are so worked up or have cognitive impairments such that teaching seems impossible. Others might feel put off by an offer to build skills. If they aren't receptive, do not teach! Also, it is important to be cognizant of the importance of self-determination and facilitative conflict consulting even during the teaching phase. This is not your time to tell them what to do or to lecture. This is the time to ask questions like: "What do you think Joe's side of the story is?" You can then follow that up with an invitation to role play Joe. You can say, "I am going to be you for a moment, and I would like you to be Joe. Tell me your story, Joe, and I will respond."

In a two-hour session, do not expect to have an ambitious teaching plan. Often the storytelling/emotional venting stage of the session takes more than half of the session. You need at least half an hour to draft and write up the conflict action plan. That might leave you with half an hour for the skills-building phase. You might want to offer the participant any of the following suggestions:

- Tips for having a difficult conversation (see Chapter Nine)
- Listening skills (reflecting, summarizing, reframing) (this chapter)
- Understanding another's perspective (this chapter)
- Role playing and reverse role playing
- Making "I" message statements (this chapter)
- Conflict mapping (see Chapter Nine)
- Basic human needs/core concerns (see Chapter Eight)

Teaching Listening Skills

Good listening is one of the essential skills needed to help a person in conflict; most of us, however, are not as proficient as we need to be. Listening is a combination of hearing what another person says, and psychological involvement with the person who is talking. Listening requires more than hearing words. It requires a desire to understand the person talking, an attitude of respect and acceptance, and a willingness to open our mind to try to see things from the point of view of the person talking. Listening requires a high level of concentration and energy. It demands that we set aside our own thoughts and agendas, put ourselves in another's shoes, and see the world through that person's eyes. True listening requires that we suspend judgment, evaluation, and approval, in an attempt to understand another's frame of reference, emotions, and attitudes.[40]

When we listen to others, we are frequently listening to our own inner dialogue and not truly being present and absorbing what the other person is saying, both through his or her words, and through body language and other communication cues. There are three levels of listening. Most of us listen at level one. When listening with the other person's interests in mind, we need to listen at level two or three.

Level One: Internal listening

When we listen at Level One, we are actually listening to the sound of our own inner voices. That's where our attention is. We may hear the words of the other person, but we are primarily aware of our own opinions, stories, judgments, feelings, needs, and itches. We may be nodding and saying, "uh huh," but inside we are saying things like: "I had an experience just like that," or "This person should really get a life," or "I'm hungry; when was the last time I ate?" or "I sure hope I say the right thing." There are plenty of times in our lives when Level One listening is appropriate. For example, when the contractor is asking how we want our kitchen remodeled; that's a situation where it is one hundred percent about what we want—our opinions, judgments, desires. And of course, it's essential that the parties in a conflict listen at level one, at least some of the time.

Level Two: Focused Listening

At Level Two, there is a hard focus, like a laser from mediator to party. All of the attention is directed in one way. Think of a parent with a sick

---

40 Rod Windle and Suzanne Warren, the National Center on Dispute Resolution in Special Education, www.directionservice.org/cadre/index.cfm (Accessed February 2012).

baby: all of his or her attention is hard focused on the child. There might be great chaos all around, but the parent stays focused on the child and the child's needs. Picture two young lovers sitting on a park bench; they're both at Level Two with their attention completely focused on the other, oblivious to the world around them. They are two people completely at Level Two; listening intently to every word and listening for every nuance in the conversation. In order for conflict resolution to be as effective as possible, those helping people in conflict need to be able to listen at Level Two.

Level Three: Global Listening

This is the soft-focus listening that takes in everything. At Level Three, we are aware of the energy between us and others. We are also aware of how that energy is changing; we detect sadness, lightness, and shifts in attitude. We are aware of the environment and whatever is going on in the environment. We are conscious of underlying mood, tone, or impact of the conversation. Stand-up comedians have a highly developed sense of listening at Level Three. They know when their humor is landing and when it isn't. This is also the level at which our intuition will be most available to us. Conflict consultants often listen at this level in order to pick up as much information as possible about the underlying impact the parties are experiencing.

What is a good listener?

So, what are characteristics of a good listener? A good listener is committed to listening; it takes practice and true commitment. A good listener needs to be willing to suspend judgment, let go of the need to fix the problem, and check for understanding.

Active listening is a significant skill that involves not only our ability to hear, but also to see, feel, and stay attentive to the other person. There are some deterrents to active listening, which include these behaviors:

- Assuming in advance that the subject is uninteresting and unimportant.
- Mentally criticizing the speaker's delivery.
- Getting over-stimulated when questioning or opposing an idea, overreacting to certain words and phrases.
- Rehearsing a response.
- Listening only for facts.
- Withdrawing attention or daydreaming.

Good listening involves listening actively, with an open mind, and may also involve summarizing, paraphrasing, restating, reflecting feeling, and reframing. Each of these tools is explained below.

Summarizing, Paraphrasing, Restating, Reflecting Feeling, and Reframing

Summarizing, paraphrasing, restating, reflecting feeling, and reframing are forms of reflective listening. By reflecting back to the speaker what we believe we understand, we validate that person by giving the person the experience of being heard and acknowledged. We also provide an opportunity for the speaker to give us feedback about the accuracy of our perceptions, thereby increasing the effectiveness of our overall communication. It is natural to shy away from using these tools out of fear of getting it wrong. However, even if we do get it wrong, the speaker will correct us and this will reinforce that the person has been heard.

Summarizing. Summarizing is a method in which we take what we have heard and distill the key points. The listener pulls together the main ideas and feelings of the speaker to show understanding. We might focus on the key concerns, point out areas of potential agreement, or organize information into topic areas. This skill is used after a considerable amount of information sharing has gone on and shows that the listener grasps the total meaning of the message. It also helps the speaker gain an integrated picture of what she or he has been saying. "You're frustrated and angry that the landlord has taken so long to respond to you and confused about why the response was to serve you with an eviction notice. You are willing to pay your rent and have prided yourself on being a good tenant. You are worried that the landlord is using you as an example for the other tenants."

Paraphrasing. This is a concise statement of the content of the speaker's message. A paraphrase should be brief, succinct, and focus on the facts or ideas of the message rather than the feeling. The paraphrase should be in the listener's own words rather than "parroting back," using the speaker's words. "You want your former employer to develop policies so that others won't be treated the way you feel you were treated." Or "You would like your landlord to provide you with an emergency number so that you do not need to take crisis situations into your own hands."

Reflecting feeling. The listener concentrates on the feeling words and asks, "How would I be feeling if I were having that experience?" The person then restates or paraphrases the feeling of what was heard in a manner that conveys understanding. "You are very worried about the impact that a door without a lock would have on your family." "You are frustrated because other students seem to be getting better treatment than you feel you are receiving."

Restating. Restating is a powerful tool, but it should be used sparingly; essentially, restating is "parroting" back exactly what we heard. It may be that the party will get annoyed and respond, "Isn't that what I just said?" This helps to double-check understanding as well as to let the other person know he or she is being heard. It also helps the party to hear another person say what the party is feeling. "You said you were fired from your job and your former employer had no procedure in place to notify employees when they are being let go." "You had a broken front door lock, and you could not reach your landlord so you fixed it and paid for it yourself."

Reframing. Reframing is perhaps the most powerful of the reflective listening tools, but it may be necessary to ask a few questions before we are able to reframe what has been said. When reframing, we take a statement or position and make it neutral or positive; we may also depersonalize it and make it noninflammatory. "Reframing means looking for constructive ways to describe, or 'frame,' whatever is going on, with the goal of changing perceptions and positions from negative and fixed to more positive and flexible."[41]

People in conflict often state their position on a particular topic. In order for them to move forward, they might need to examine what interest is underneath the position. A position is a specific solution that a person proposes or demands. For example, one person insists, "I'm sick of her closing the window; I want it open," and the other replies, "You only think of yourself; I want the window closed."

In order to reframe these statements, each speaker might be asked what he or she needs or is interested in. The answer for one may be a need for fresh air in order to feel awake and healthy. The other may respond that he or she is feeling chilled following a recent illness and needs a warm environment. The listener may reflect to each of them, "You are interested in health and well-being?" By reframing each of the positional statements, the listener has helped the speakers see that they have a common interest and therefore may be able to come up with a win-win solution.

Here are some questions to ask in order to get at underlying interests:

---

41 Wilmot and Hocker, 259.

1. Why is that important to you?
2. What matters to you most?
3. Can you say more about your basic concerns with this?
4. Can you say more about what seems unfair here?
5. What is it that concerns you about this?
6. What leads you to say that?
7. Can you say more about how you see things?
8. What information might you have that would help make understanding more clear?
9. What specific information is in your mind about this?
10. What past experiences influence how you're thinking about this?

As stated earlier, when we listen to someone in conflict, it is best to listen at Level Three—be a global listener. It is a good idea to listen for these characteristics:

- Interests
- Values
- Agreements
- Disagreement
- Ideas
- Information
- Sticking Points

We can listen attentively and patiently to people even if they are saying something we disagree with. With careful listening, we learn information that is valuable to understanding the problem as the other person sees it. We gain a greater understanding of the other person's perception. When we have a deeper understanding of another's perception, whether we agree with it or not, we hold the key to understanding that person's motivation, attitude, and behavior. We have a deeper understanding of the problem and the potential paths for reaching agreement.[42]

Rod Windle and Suzanne Warren, in an article[43] for the National Center on Dispute Resolution in Special Education, state that a good listener must focus on the following tips in order to improve listening skills:

Nonverbal

- Give full physical attention to the speaker.
- Being aware of the speaker's nonverbal messages.

Verbal

- Pay attention to the words *and* feelings that are being expressed.
- Use reflective listening tools such as paraphrasing, reflecting, summarizing, and questioning to increase understanding of the message and help the speaker tell his or her story.

Giving Full Physical Attention to the Speaker

Attending is the art and skill of giving full, physical attention to another person. In his book *People Skills*, Robert Bolton Ph.D. refers to "listening with the whole body."

Effective attending is a careful balance of alertness and relaxation that includes appropriate body movement, eye contact, and "posture of involvement." Fully attending says to the speaker, "What you are saying is very important. I am totally present and intent on understanding you." We create a posture of involvement by doing the following:

---

42 Windle and Warren. www.directionservice.org/cadre/index.cfm (Accessed February 2012).
43 Ibid.

- Lean gently toward the speaker.
- Face the speaker squarely.
- Maintain an open posture with arms and legs uncrossed.
- Maintain an appropriate distance from the speaker.
- Move our bodies in response to the speaker, e.g., appropriate head nodding and facial expressions.

When we pay attention to a speaker's body language we gain insight into how that person is feeling as well as the intensity of the feeling. Through careful attention to body language and paraverbal messages, we are able to develop hunches about what the speaker (or listener) is communicating. We can then, through our reflective listening skills, check the accuracy of those hunches by expressing in our own words our impression of what is being communicated.

Paying Attention to the Words and Feelings

In order to understand the total meaning of a message, we must be able to gain understanding about both the *feeling* and the *content* of the message. We are often more comfortable dealing with the content rather than the feelings (e.g., the relationship), particularly when the feelings are intense. Our tendency is to try to ignore the emotional aspect of the message/conflict and move directly to the substance of the issues. This can lead to an escalation of intense emotions. It may be necessary to deal directly with the relationship problem by openly acknowledging and naming the feelings and having an honest discussion about them prior to moving into the substantive issues. If we leave the emotional aspect unaddressed, we risk missing important information about the problem, as well as derailing the communication process.

> "In order to understand the total meaning of a message, we must be able to gain understanding about both the *feeling* and the *content* of the message."

"Listening in dialogue is listening more to meaning than to words…In true listening, we reach behind the words, see through them, to find the person who is being revealed. Listening is a search to find the treasure of the true person as revealed verbally and non-verbally. There is the semantic problem, of course. The words bear a different connotation for you than they do for me. Consequently, I can never tell you what you said, but only what I heard. I will have to rephrase what you have said, and check it out with you to make sure that what left your mind and heart arrived in my mind and heart intact and without distortion."

—John Powell, theologian

"I" Messages

We can use "I" messages to take responsibility for our own feelings in conflict situations. Generally beginning with the word "I," these statements offer an alternative to the more destructive "You" messages, which attack, blame, or criticize someone else. For example, "I" messages allow us to say, "I'm angry about this mess," *instead of* "You kids are such inconsiderate slobs!" *or* "You make me so angry!" "I" messages break down barriers, allowing us to listen to each other. "You" messages put up walls because we are busy defending ourselves from attack.

"I" messages simply state a problem without blaming someone for it. This makes it easier for the participants in the conflict to help solve the problem, without having to admit that they were wrong. An "I" message has a greater likelihood of motivating others to change their behavior when it is unacceptable. It also protects their self-esteem, preserves the relationship, facilitates a better understanding of what is going on in the relationship, and improves performance.[44] "I" messages

---

44 The websites http://www.only-effective-communication-skills.com/imessages and http://www.crinfo.org/CK_Essays/ck_iu_messages.jsp have excellent definitions (Accessed February 2012).

can be used to explain our concern when we own a problem, and other types of "I" messages can be used to share our views and feelings when there is no problem.

"I" messages usually contain three elements:

1. A description of the behavior—what actually happened.
2. The concrete, tangible effects of that behavior on ME.
3. How I feel about the behavior and its effects.

We may be very angry about the other person's behavior, but we remain focused on the issue we are angry about.

"I" statements were originally studied by Dr. Haim Ginott, a noted psychologist who discerned that statements starting with "I" tended to be less provocative than those starting with "you." It isn't necessary to always start a sentence with "I," but the focus needs to be on how we feel about a situation, clearly stated, and not on how terrible the other is for causing it. Along these lines, psychologist John Gottman, one of this country's foremost relationship scientists, points to the importance of introducing our complaints in a "softer" noncritical, noncontemptuous way if we are to obtain resolution.

By using "I" statements, conflicts are less likely to escalate and relationships are more likely to improve. In other words, if we say "I felt let down," rather than "You broke your promise," we will convey the same information, but we will do so in a way that is less likely to provoke a defensive or hostile reaction from our opponent. "You" messages suggest blame, and encourage the recipient to deny wrongdoing or blame back. For example, if we say "you broke your promise," the answer is likely to be "No, I didn't," which sets us up for a lengthy argument, or "Well, you did, too," which also continues the conflict.

In addition, when we are in conflict, especially an escalated conflict, there is a very strong tendency to blame many of our problems on the other person. So stating the problem in terms of a "you" message is much more natural, and is more consistent with our view of the problem. But by making the effort to change our language, we can also reframe the way we think about the conflict, increasing the likelihood that a resolution can be found.[45]

Remembering to use "I" messages can be difficult, however, because many people are not used to talking about themselves or their feelings (and in some cultures, this would be highly inappropriate). In addition, when we are in conflict, especially an escalated conflict, there is a very strong tendency to blame many of our problems on the other side. So stating the problem in terms of a "you" message is much more natural, and is more consistent with our view of the problem. But by making the effort to change our language, we can also reframe the way we think about the conflict, increasing the likelihood that a resolution can be found.[46]

The exercise on the following page can be instructional for a participant who needs some help understanding how to transform his or her statements into an "I" message.

---

45 http://www.crinfo.org/CK_Essays/ck_iu_messages.jsp (Accessed February 2012).
46 Ibid.

Exercise: Practicing "I" Statements

Change each example below into an "I" statement using the following format:

I feel _____ *when you [do]* _____ *because* _____ *. I would like you to* _____ *.*

Scenario	Original Statement	"I" Statement
1. Your neighbor played loud music until 2:00 a.m.	You are a lousy neighbor and care only about yourself!	
2. Your landlord doesn't respond to your requests for repairs.	You care more about money than people and are a slum lord.	
3. Your friend was not paying attention when you were speaking about your new job yesterday at dinner.	You never listen to a single thing anyone else says.	
4. Your coworker ate all the cookies you brought for the entire office.	You are the most selfish person I've ever met.	
5. Last week your friend gave you a used birthday card for your birthday.	You are so cheap you make Scrooge look like a generous person.	
6. You came home last night and your kids left dirty dishes all over the kitchen.	You kids are lazy slobs. Why can't you help out and clean up?	
7. You took your significant other on a trip and s/he complained about the accommodations, food, activities, etc.	You get on my nerves with your constant complaining	
8. Your ex-wife returned the kids to you late and the kids were hungry and unclean.	You are an unfit mother. I am going to get full custody of the kids.	
9. Your friend did not pay you back for the concert ticket you paid for with your credit card.	You always borrow money and never pay back what you borrowed	
10. [Use an example from your own experience]	[Use an example from your own experience]	

Fig. 15

Role Playing and Reverse Role Playing

Role playing allows participants to take risk-free positions by acting out characters in hypothetical situations. Role playing is an enlightening and interesting way to help people see a problem from another perspective. It can help them understand the range of concerns, values, and positions held by other people. Simply put, role playing is a rehearsal. Many of us use role play as a basic tool of life. Whenever we project into the future in a kind of "what if" scenario we are indulging in a role play of some sort, we are projecting ourselves into an imaginary situation where, though we cannot control the outcome, we can anticipate some or all of the conditions and "rehearse" our performance in order to influence the outcome. Much of the time we are better for it. By way of example, you might wish to speak to your mechanic because he or she has not addressed the strange noise your car is making. Before doing so you might rehearse to yourself what you intend to say. This would be a mini role play; we do it all the time because it helps.

If a participant is having difficulty seeing the perspective of the other party, you might want to have the participant play the other person. This scenario will force the person into the other person's shoes for a moment. For example, Pete came in complaining that his landlord is never around, doesn't return phone calls, and doesn't make repairs in a timely fashion. He was very upset about the holes in his walls and the over-heating in the winter. He wishes he could move, but the rent is very reasonable and he feels stuck. When the conflict consultant said, "Okay, Pete, I am you, and you are the landlord; let's talk," here's what happened:

Pete (played by conflict consultant): "I am sick and tired of this dump I live in. I can never get in touch with you and you're being very irresponsible."

Landlord (played by Pete): "You are lucky you have a place to live! The rent is cheap and you stay warm in the winter! I should have raised my rent years ago! You have the cheapest place in town!"

Pete: "You have to make repairs. I know my rights."

Landlord: "Yes, but there is nothing I can do about the heating system without tearing it out and starting all over again, and then I might as well tear down the whole building."

Pete: "Well, then I would have no place to live!"

Landlord: "Exactly. I want my tenants to have a safe and cheap place to live. I am sorry I have not fixed the holes. I had to let the repairman go because I don't have the money to pay him. I will try to get over there after work tonight."

At this point in the role play, Pete's entire demeanor changed. He looked at the conflict consultant and said, "I never looked at it that way."

The conflict consultant said, "What way?"

"From his world. He works two jobs and tries to manage this big old apartment building himself. A lot of the other buildings have been torn down or fixed up so much that no one can afford the rent. I guess I should have tried to make a specific time for him to come fix the holes instead of getting so angry and feeling so sorry for myself. I really am glad I have a cheap place to live; it really is a nice place."

After this role play, Pete felt ready to call the landlord and ask for a specific day and time to have the holes fixed. He practiced some "I" message statements and worked on what he would do if the landlord did not fix the holes by the end of the month. He left the session with a written action plan and felt more hopeful and grateful.

Putting Yourself in Their Shoes: Seeking Other Perspectives

Henry Ford said this about success: "If there is any one secret of success, it lies in the ability to get the other person's point of view and see things from that person's angle as well as from your own."

Our perspective on anything is shaped by our beliefs, values, and experience. Adopting another's perspective is learned behavior; human beings are not born with the capacity to recognize another's perspective; rather, this is developed during the first few years of life.[47]

Just as there are two or more sides to every story, there are plenty of different ideas on what is right and what is wrong. No one person has a corner on that market. Consider Harvey Mackay's story of three people who looked at the Grand Canyon:

The priest said, "What a glory of God!"

The geologist said, "What a wonder of science!"

The cowboy said, "What an awful place to lose a horse!"[48] Harvey Mackay writes, "How we approach an issue often colors our thinking about the result we wish to achieve. What we want may not line up with the next person's desired outcome. Our motives are not wrong, just very different. We need to respect and consider that our own views may not be the only one with real merit."

"Will Rogers, a uniquely American humorist known for his homespun wisdom and wit, summed up perspective this way: 'You must never disagree with a man while you are facing him. Go around behind him and look the same way he is looking and you will see that things look different from what they do when you're facing him. Look over his shoulder and get his viewpoint, then go back and face him and you will have a different idea.'"[49]

Humans are capable of adopting another's perspective and considering another's thoughts, feelings, and mental states. Possessing this capability does not, however, mean that people

---

47 Nicholas Caruso and Eugene M. Eply, "Perspective Taking: Misstepping into Others' Shoes." *Handbook of Imagination and Mental Simulation*, edited by K. D. Markman, W. M. Klein, and J. A. Suhr. New York: Psychology Press, 2009.

48 Used with permission from Harvey Mackay, Harvey@mackay.com. Column distributed by United Feature Syndicate.

49 Ibid.

will necessarily use their perspective-taking skills when they should, or that their skills will actually lead them to accurately identify another person's mental states. Recent advancements in research on the processes underlying perspective taking, in fact, suggest several important challenges to using our perspective-taking capabilities to their fullest potential and demonstrate a series of reliable missteps that happen when stepping (or failing to step) into others' shoes. Some people are, at times, too heavily influenced by their own egocentric viewpoint. And, even when they manage to step beyond their own perspective, they may trip over the inaccurate or incomplete information on which they rely when intuiting another's mind.[50]

What is needed in order to see another's perspective is empathy and a desire to treat that person favorably. We may need to suppress our usual selfish behavior and have a heightened desire to help the other person. Research consistently demonstrates that when people are able to take another person's perspective, they become more compassionate and empathetic, often resulting in offers to help the person whose perspective was taken. However, perspective taking can also be used for malevolent purposes (e.g., anticipating a rival's next move and taking steps to thwart it).

Perspective taking is the ability to see things from another person's point of view. Perspective taking involves two factors: (1) cognitive, how a person thinks about a given situation; and (2) affective, how a person feels about the situation. Both of these factors also induce people's behavior. Conflict resolution consulting involves helping the participant explore how his or her actions are impacting the other party.[51]

"The essence of perspective taking is demonstrating understanding. In conflict, when one conveys an understanding of another's point of view or feelings, it begins to loosen the jam of opposing positions. It

---

50 Caruso and Eply.

51 Used with permission of the Good Shepherd Mediation Program Conflict Resolution Coaching 2009 Training Manual.

quite literally shows a respect for the other's comprehension of a situation or response to it. When we work with those who are in conflict, we might ask them to focus on perspective taking to the satisfaction of their opponent. In other words, the goal of perspective taking becomes the conveyance of the conflict partner's position or emotions so well that the parties are convinced that there is a shared understanding. When this occurs, the chance that the conflict can result in a constructive outcome, though not assured, is extraordinarily improved."[52]

Sometimes it is useful to show the following pictures to people who are having trouble seeing the other's perspective. What do they see in picture number one—a vase, or two profiles facing each other? How about picture number two—is this an old woman or a young woman? Is it possible both perspectives are correct?

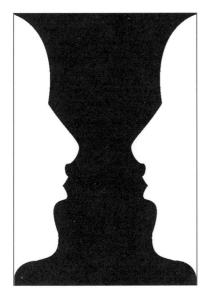

Fig. 16

Fig. 17

"We don't see things as they are; we see things as we are."

—Anais Nin

---

52 Tim Flanagan and Craig Runde. *Perspective Taking* (January 2007) http://www.mediate.com/articles/rundeC3.cfm (Accessed February 2012).

Chapter Twelve

Understanding Forgiveness and Empathy

One might suggest that parties in conflict are incapable of showing empathy for one another or forgiving the other person. A person coming to conflict consulting is usually very distressed; are empathy and forgiveness really viable topics for consideration? According to the *Merriam-Webster Dictionary*, empathy is "the action of understanding, being aware of, and being sensitive to, and vicariously experiencing the feelings, thoughts, and experience of another of either the past or present without having the feelings, thoughts, and experience fully communicated in an objectively explicit manner." Even though a conflict resolution consultant may not explicitly ask a participant to be empathetic to the other party, that is the goal.

Transformation happens when participants move beyond simply hearing and understanding the others' perspective toward truly empathizing. Proponents of empathic mediation contend that "beneath the positions and strategies of people in conflict lies a magnetic field of possibility, our common humanity, ready to invite resolution. Empathic mediation is a structure for resolving conflict that taps into this rich source of resolution with empathy." Using the skills of empathic communication, the mediator creates a safe and balanced environment in which people can be heard as they wish to be heard. This model differs from other structures for negotiation in that strategic thinking is delayed until after empathic connection has been established between the participants. Empathic mediation can be used on its own or in conjunction with other conventional mediation techniques.

Empathy is the ability to project oneself into the personality of another person in order to better understand that person's emotions or feelings. The empathic listener lets the speaker know, "I understand your problem and how you feel about it; I am interested in what you are saying and I am not judging you." The listener unmistakably conveys this message through words and nonverbal behaviors, including body language. In so doing, the listener encourages the speaker to fully express herself or himself free of interruption, criticism, or being told what to do. It is neither advisable nor necessary for a conflict consultant to agree with the speaker, even when asked to do so. It is usually sufficient to let the speaker know, "I understand you, and I am interested in being a resource to help you resolve this problem." Empathic listening is a core skill that is necessary both for the conflict consultant as well as for the participant. The consultant models this skill the following ways:

> "Empathy is the ability to project oneself into the personality of another person in order to better understand that person's emotions or feelings."

1. Let the participant (not the consultant) dominate the discussion.
2. Be attentive to what is being said.
3. No interrupting.
4. Use open-ended questions.
5. Show sensitivity to the emotions being expressed.
6. Reflect back to the participant what feelings or content the person expressed.

The power of empathic listening in volatile settings is reflected in Madelyn Burley-Allen's description of the skilled listener: "When you listen well, you…

1. acknowledge the speaker;
2. increase the speaker's self-esteem and confidence;
3. tell the speaker, 'You are important' and 'I am not judging you';
4. gain the speaker's cooperation;
5. reduce stress and tension;
6. build teamwork;
7. gain trust;
8. elicit openness;
9. gain a sharing of ideas and thoughts; and
10. obtain more valid information about the speakers and the subject."[53]

To obtain these results, Burley-Allen says, a skilled listener…

1. "takes information from others while remaining nonjudgmental and empathic;
2. acknowledges the speaker in a way that invites the communication to continue; and
3. provides a limited but encouraging response, carrying the speaker's idea one step forward."[54]

Before a consultant can expect an emotionally distraught party to give clear and accurate information about the conflict, the consultant must enable that party to engage in a cathartic process, according to Lyman S. Steil.[55] A former president of the American Listening

---

53 Madelyn Burley-Allen, *Listening: The Forgotten Skills* (John Wiley & Sons, 1995).

54 Ibid.

55 On Listening…and Not Listening, *Executive Health* (newsletter, 1981). See also, *Effective Listening* by Steil, Barker, and Watson (McGraw Hill, 1983) and *Listening Leaders* (Beaver's Pond Press, 2004).

Association defined catharsis as "the process of releasing emotion, the ventilation of feelings, the sharing of problems or frustrations with an empathic listener. "Catharsis," he continues, "basically requires an understanding listener who is observant to the cathartic need cues and clues. People who need catharsis will often give verbal and nonverbal cues, and good listeners will be sensitive enough to recognize them. Cathartic fulfillment is necessary for maximized success at all other levels of communication."

"Cathartic communication," Steil continues, "requires caring, concerned, risk-taking and nonjudgmental listening. Truly empathic people suspend evaluation and criticism when they listen to others. Here the challenge is to enter into the private world of the speaker, to understand without judging actions or feelings."

Being willing to apologize is a key component in empathy. Seiji Takaku produced a report under the title, "The effects of apology and perspective taking on interpersonal forgiveness."[56] Takaku's research offers important insights on how apologies work. Mutual empathy is key. While the offer of an apology may be the result of, and an expression of, the offender's empathy with the offended party, forgiveness requires empathy from the offended to the offender. Empathy must be experienced by, and communicated by, both parties to the conflict, not simply one or the other. In other words, to be effective in resolving conflict, apology and forgiveness are best viewed as interactive processes, not simply one-sided speech events. Takaku's research demonstrates that an offended party has the power to shift the nature of a conflict interaction by reflecting on his or her own "imperfect nature," developing empathy for the offender, and thus being open to the process of apology and forgiveness.

Forgiveness is a close cousin to empathy. Being willing to forgive, as well as forgiving another who you believe has harmed you, are transfor-

---

56 The report appeared in the *Journal of Social Psychology*, 141(4), 494–508.

mational components of conflict resolution. In an article "The Necessity of Forgiveness," Dr. Fred Luskin defines forgiveness: "to forgive is to give up all hope for a better past. If you are locked in regret over the past, you have less available to your life now. The other problem is that if you don't forgive, then you are in some ways prejudging your future—that you are on guard and defended and helpless, that there's a residual bitterness that influences your capacity for happiness because you haven't resolved something from your past."

Dr. Luskin continues, "Forgiveness allows you a fresh start, whether it's a big insult or a small one. It's like a rain coming to a polluted environment. It clears things. At some point, you can say that this awful thing happened to me. It hurt like hell, yet I'm not going to allow it to take over my life. That's the choice that's always available. When you're with someone who's had tragedy, you offer that choice, although you don't tell them to take it. Without it, they can get stuck in bitterness and revenge. That's the cost of not forgiving. When you meet people who have forgiven, you see their power. You see the strength and courage it takes to forgive in a world dominated by an eye for an eye."

> "Forgiveness allows you a fresh start, whether it's a big insult or a small one."

"There's clear evidence that if people apologize, it's easier to forgive. Forgiveness, though, is not limited by that. You can forgive even if the person utters no conciliatory words and suffers no consequence, because forgiveness is always for you. You forgive by remembering what happened and you commit yourself to it never happening again. Or, you can remember it and say, 'I'm not going to suffer any more. I'm going to bring some goodness to the people in my life.' It's an active quality. It has nothing to do with forgetting. And it's a very powerful statement."[57]

---

57 Taken from http://www.pbs.org/kqed/onenight/stories/forgive/index.html. (Accessed February 2012).

Nine Steps to Forgiveness

by Frederic Luskin, Ph.D. (reprinted with permission)

1. Know exactly how you feel about what happened and be able to articulate what about the situation is not okay. Then, tell a trusted couple of people about your experience.

2. Make a commitment to yourself to do what you have to do to feel better. Forgiveness is for you and not for anyone else.

3. Forgiveness does not necessarily mean reconciliation with the people who hurt you, or condoning of their action. What you are after is to find peace. Forgiveness can be defined as the "peace and understanding that come from blaming that which has hurt you less, taking the life experience less personally, and changing your grievance story."

4. Get the right perspective on what is happening. Recognize that your primary distress is coming from the hurt feelings, thoughts, and physical upset you are suffering now, not what offended you or hurt you two minutes—or ten years ago. Forgiveness helps to heal those hurt feelings.

5. At the moment you feel upset, practice a simple stress management technique to soothe your body's flight or fight response.

6. Give up expecting things from your life, or from other people who may choose not to do what you expect them to do. Recognize the "unenforceable rules" you have for your health or how you or other people must behave. Remind yourself that you can hope for health, love, peace, and prosperity, and work hard to get them.

7. Put your energy into looking for another way to get your positive goals met than through the experience that has hurt you. Instead of mentally replaying your hurt, seek out new ways to get what you want.

8. Remember that a life well lived is your best revenge. Instead of focusing on your wounded feelings, and thereby giving the person who caused you pain power over you, learn to look for the love, beauty, and kindness around you. Forgiveness is about personal power.

9. Amend your grievance story to remind you of the heroic choice to forgive. The practice of forgiveness has been shown to reduce anger, hurt, depression, and stress, and leads to greater feelings of hope, peace, compassion, and self-confidence. Practicing forgiveness leads to healthy relationships as well as physical health. It also influences our attitude which opens the heart to kindness, beauty, and love.[58]

---

58 http://learningtoforgive.com (Accessed February 2012). Used with permission.

Chapter Thirteen

Developing an Action Plan

The final stage of the conflict resolution consulting process calls for building a plan of action and, if desired, writing up a conflict action plan. This may be the time to do reality testing, summarize all issues, and double-check that all have been discussed. This is not the time, however, to make recommendations or offer your ideas for solutions. This is the time to ask, "What do you want your next steps to be?"

> "The final stage of the conflict resolution consulting process calls for building a plan of action."

In a group setting, when people are addressing difficult issues, they might brainstorm to come up with possibilities. Brainstorming is a group problem-solving technique that involves the spontaneous contribution of ideas from all members of the group. It can also be the mulling over of ideas by one individual in an attempt to devise or find a solution to a problem. You can ask participants if they can brainstorm all the possibilities and remind them that these possible solutions don't have to be realistic or well thought out. In brainstorming we often say, "No idea is stupid." You could offer to write down all the ideas the participant has, encouraging this process until all possibilities have been exhausted. You can then go over each one and ask questions such as:

"Why did you come up with this one?" "Explain this more." "What do you think the outcome might be if you went with this one?" "How realistic is this one?" You can go through a process of elimination until the participant comes up with one or more steps/solutions the person is willing and able to pursue.

Some people cannot brainstorm or are very uncomfortable with the process. If they are truly unsure what their next steps should be, you can ask, "Can you think of someone who might be able to help you decide what to do next?" or "Are there legal issues that you need help with?" It is important that every conflict consultant have a comprehensive list of referrals and resources to give to every participant as needed. The list should include services such as legal advice, courts, crime prevention and victim assistance, counseling, children services, family services, housing resources, socials services, elder resources, and city, county, and state resources. An action plan might simply include the next resource the person plans to contact to address the conflict. A participant may decide to do any of the following as a result of a conflict consulting session:

- Talk to the person.
- Write a letter.
- Talk to a professional.
- Return for another conflict consultation.
- Request that the other party attend mediation.
- Call the police.
- File a lawsuit.
- Ignore the problem.
- Move away.

If the participant decides to talk directly to the person involved in the conflict, you will want to discuss seeking a safe environment. Discuss where to address the other person involved in terms of a neutral turf, convenience, safety, privacy, and how to eliminate distractions.

Discuss the benefits and obstacles of each place, if necessary. You will want to cover how soon to address the other person. Has there been a sufficient cooling-off period? How much time should be scheduled? Discuss ground rules to minimize the chance of escalating the situation (e.g., one person speaks at a time; respect each other's point of view). Ask the participant what she or he can do to make the other person comfortable. Make sure the participant has plans for informing the other person that there is an important issue to be discussed, and asking when it would be a good time to get together to speak privately.

If the participant is going to have a conversation with the other party, prepare the participant to listen actively to the other person. Did you discuss active listening skills (e.g., open body language, paraphrasing)? You should be prepared to discuss the importance of using "I" messages to express concerns. You might also ask the participant to predict possible responses from the other person and practice responding, especially to the dreaded questions. Have you adequately practiced areas of concern and things that may be difficult to hear or talk about? As mentioned earlier, you might brainstorm ideas for resolution without judging whether they will work. You could point out pitfalls of insufficient brainstorming and premature evaluation. You can ask the participant to evaluate those options to see how they might play out if selected (e.g., reality test possible consequences). Also important is identifying and discussing what the participant will do if the discussion does not result in a resolution (e.g., let it go, mediate, litigate). The action plan you and the participant come up with will be a kind of to-do list, including the commitments the participant made to address the conflict constructively. The plan of action should be in the participant's own words. You can write down what the person says, but it is important that the words come from the participant. You might also want to arrange for a follow-up appointment or phone call to see how things worked out. See Appendix A for sample templates for conflict resolution action plans.

Final Words

Moving Ahead

Chances are you are well aware of how divided we are in many areas of our world. From family and friendship to government and international relations, we separate ourselves from others because we are sure our interests, needs, values, beliefs, and morals do not line up with theirs. We are often more interested in being "right" than we are in having peace. We make assumptions about other people that are not always grounded in fact. We are capable of talking about what bothers us with regard to another person, as long as it is not communicated right to the person's face. The concepts explained in this book seem so simple, yet they are truly underutilized.

How different our world would be if each of us had a collaborative conversation with those we opposed, and if we used focused listening, clarifying questions, summarizing, reframing, and checking for the other perspective in our conversations. If we focused on our interests instead of on our positions and looked for areas of commonality, wouldn't we find more peace in our relationships as well as in our world affairs? This book and the Conflict Resolution Center's Conflict Resolution Consulting Program were developed because of a strong belief that face-to-face dialogue through mediation, conflict resolution consulting, and other forms of facilitation are the preferred methods of obtaining justice and relief from conflict. Our hope is that this book will be used in multiple areas by people who encounter difficult relationships. We hope the tools will be passed along from everyone in a position to help others resolve conflict. If you are a peacemaker and want others to also learn the skills of peacemaking, share the skills and pass this book along. For more information, or if you wish to learn to serve as a conflict resolution consultant, contact the Conflict Resolution Center at 612-822-9883 www.crcminnesota.org.

Appendix A

Sample Action Plans

Conflict Action Plan

Summary of Conflict:

How I would like to see this resolved:

Skills I Learned Today:
- ☐ "I" statements
- ☐ How I resolve conflict
- ☐ Listening tips
- ☐ Conflict resolution tips
- ☐ De-escalating
- ☐ Forgiveness
- ☐ Perspectives
- ☐ Other

People I Need to Talk to About This:

When I Will Talk to Them:

Services/Organizations I Need to Contact:

When I Will Do This:

What Information I Need:

When I Will Get This Information:

I Plan to:
- ☐ Talk to [the party]:
- ☐ Write a letter
- ☐ Talk to a professional (specify):
- ☐ Return for another conflict consultation
- ☐ Ask the other party to attend mediation
- ☐ Call the police
- ☐ File a lawsuit
- ☐ Other

Participant_____   Date:_____

Conflict Plan of Action

As a result of conflict consulting held on ____/____/____, this is how I plan to address the conflict situation.

When: _____

Where: _____

Ground Rules:_____

"I" Messages: _____

_____

Script: _____

_____

Issues: _____

Possible Solutions: _____

_____

Best Alternative: _____

Other: _____

_____

Participant_____   Date:_____

Participant_____   Date:_____

Appendix B

Conflict Resolution Consultant's Checklist

(Adapted from Good Shepherd Mediation Program training Manual, 2009)

Introduction—Consultant's Opening Statement

☐ Define "conflict consulting" and your role as a "consultant."

☐ Review how the process works.

☐ Explain confidentiality and exclusions.

☐ Discuss housekeeping logistics.

Emotional Expression/Storytelling

☐ Storytelling: Ask the person experiencing conflict to describe the situation.

☐ Visioning: Discuss the participant's goals. What is the participant's ideal outcome?

☐ Positively reframe negative self-talk associated with the story.

Conflict Assessment

☐ How have you tried to address this situation in the past?

☐ What was (were) the outcome(s)?

☐ Were you happy with the outcome(s)?

☐ Is there any reason to believe that if you continue doing what you have been, you will get different results?

☐ What other ways could you respond?

☐ What could you do differently?

☐ What would you like to see happen as an outcome?

Skills Building

(The following are suggestions only. You will not be
able to do many of these in one two-hour session.)

Perspective Taking

- ☐ Ask: How does the other person view the situation?
- ☐ If the participant does not appear to be able to "walk in the other person's shoes," ask the participant to tell the story from the other person's perspective (role reversal).
- ☐ Explore the conflict in terms of the participant's and the other's identity (threats).
- ☐ Explore the conflict in terms of the participant's and the other's emotions.
- ☐ Explore the conflict in terms of the participant's and the other's power.

Conflict Styles

- ☐ Have the participant take the *Thomas-Kilmann Conflict Styles Inventory*.
- ☐ Explain the conflict styles.
- ☐ Discuss the participant's perception of the other person's conflict resolution style in relation to the participant.
- ☐ Look at which style might be most appropriate in the instant situation (given the participant's style and the other's style).
  - ✓ Is the relationship important?
  - ✓ Is the issue important?
  - ✓ Is the timing right?
  - ✓ Is there room for give and take?
  - ✓ What is the level of trust between the parties?

Clarify Issues, Positions, Interests, & Common Ground

- ☐ List concerns (issues from the person's perspective).
- ☐ Identify positions (wants).
- ☐ Identify the participant's interests (needs).
- ☐ Encourage perspective taking (e.g., Why do you think the other person is behaving that way?)
- ☐ Identify the other person's positions (use role reversal).
- ☐ Identify the other person's needs (use role reversal).
- ☐ Frame issues in a neutral manner.
- ☐ Identify common ground.

Talk About Active Listening

- ☐ Prepare participant to listen actively to the other person: discuss active listening skills (e.g., open body language, paraphrasing).
- ☐ Talk about constructing "I" messages that express the person's concerns.
- ☐ Predict possible responses from the other person and practice responding.
- ☐ Prepare responses to dreaded questions.
- ☐ Practice areas of concern: things that may be difficult to hear or talk about.

Setting the Stage For Courageous Conversations

- ☐ **Seek a safe environment**: Discuss where to address the other person involved in terms of neutral turf, convenience, safety, privacy, and how to eliminate distractions. Discuss the benefits and obstacles of each place, if necessary.
- ☐ **Timing**: Discuss when to address the other person in terms of immediacy, cooling off periods, scheduling, and how much time to block out for the meeting.

- ☐ **Guidelines**: Discuss ground rules to minimize the chance of escalating the situation (e.g., one person speaks at a time; respect each other's point of view).
- ☐ **Comfort level**: What can you do to make the other person comfortable? (e.g., refreshments, seating)
- ☐ **Other considerations**: What other environmental issues might be a consideration?
- ☐ **Ask permission**: Plans for approaching the other person, informing him or her that there is an important issue to be discussed, and asking when it would be a good time to get together to speak privately.

Empathy and Forgiveness

Discuss, if appropriate, how empathy and forgiveness fit in the situation.

Generate & Evaluate Possible Solutions

☐ Brainstorm ideas for resolution without judging whether they will work.

☐ Point out pitfalls of insufficient brainstorming and premature evaluation.

☐ Evaluate those options to see how they might play out if selected (e.g., reality test possible consequences).

Knowing When to Walk Away

☐ Identify and discuss the participant's BATNA (Best Alternative to a Negotiated Agreement).

☐ Contingency plans: Discuss other options to explore if the discussion does not result in a resolution (e.g., let it go, mediate, litigate).

The Plan of Action

☐ Draft a to-do list and include the commitments the participant made to address the conflict constructively.

☐ Review the Plan of Action with the participant.

☐ Provide a list of resources.

☐ Schedule a follow-up appointment/phone call to see how things worked out (optional).

☐ Affirm and encourage the participant's best efforts to address the conflict constructively.

Bibliography

Publications

American Arbitration Association (AAA), the American Bar Association (ABA), and the Society of Professionals in Dispute Resolution (SPIDR). "Model Standards of Conduct for Mediators." *ADR Bulletin*, Vol. 5, No. 3 [2002], Art. 7.

Bodtker, Andrea and Tricia Jones. "Mediating with Heart in Mind: Addressing Emotion in Mediation practice." *Negotiation Journal*, 17:3. 2001, 217–244.

"Conflict Education in a Special Needs Population," *Mediation Quarterly*, 17:217(2), 1999, 109–124.

Burley-Allen, Madelyn. *Listening: The Forgotten Skill*, John Wiley & Sons, 1982. (Burley-Allen is a former president of the American Listening Assn.)

Canary, Dan, William R. Cupach, and Susan J. Messman. *Relationship Conflict: Conflict in Parent-Child, Friendship, and Romantic Relationships.* Sage Publications, 2005.

Conflict Resolution Information Source. "I-Messages and You-Messages." 2011. http://www.crinfo.org/CK_Essays/ck_iu_ messages.jsp.

Eply, Nicholas and Eugene M. Caruso. "Perspective Taking: Misstepping into Others' Shoes." *Handbook of Imagination and*

Mental Simulation, edited by K. D. Markman, W.M. Klein, and J.A. Suhr. New York: Psychology Press, 2009, 295–309.

Fisher, Roger and Daniel Shapiro. *Beyond Reason.* Penguin Books, 2005.

Goffman, Erving. "On Facework: An analysis of ritual elements in social interaction," *Psychiatry Journal of Interpersonal Relations*, 18:3. 1955.

Goleman, Daniel. *Emotional Intelligence*: *Why it can matter more than IQ.* New York: Bantam, 1995.

Heen, Sheila, Douglas Stone, and Bruce Patton. *Difficult Conversations.* Penguin Books. 1999.

Jones, Tricia S. and Ross Brinkert. *Conflict Coaching: Conflict Management Strategies and Skills for the Individual.* Thousand Oaks, CA: Sage Publications, 2008.

Lieberman, M.D., N.I. Eisenberger, M.J. Crockett, S.M. Tom, J.H. Pfeifer, and B.M. Way. "Putting Feelings Into Words: Affect Labeling Disrupts Amygdala Activity in Response to Affective Stimuli." *Psychological Science, 18*(5), 2007, 421–28.

Luskin, Fred. *Forgive for Good.* Harper Collins, 2002.

National Center on Dispute Resolution. Last modified 2010. www.directionservice.org/cadre/index.cfm.

Noble, Cinnie. *Conflict Management Coaching: The CINERGY™ Model.* Cincinnati: Wordsworth Communications, 2012.

Runde, Craig E. and Tim A. Flanagan. *Becoming a Conflict Competent Leader: How You and Your Organization Can Manage Conflict.* Jossey-Bass, 2006.

Steil, Lyman K. "On Listening…and Not Listening," *Executive Health* (newsletter, 1981). (Dr. Steil is a former president of the American Listening Assn.) See also *Effective Listening* by Steil, Barker, and Watson, McGraw Hill, 1983, and *Listening Leaders*, Beaver's Pond Press, 2003.

Thomas, Kenneth and Ralph Kilmann. *Thomas-Kilmann Conflict Mode Instrument*—also known as the TKI (Mountain View, CA: CPP, Inc., 1974–2009) and www.kilmann.com/conflict.

Tidwell, Alan. "Problem Solving for One." *Management Development Forum* 1 (1998).

Putnam, L.L. "Communication and Interpersonal Conflict in Organizations." *Management Communication Quarterly* 3, 1988, 293–301.

Ting-Toomey, Stella and John G. Oetzel. *Managing Intercultural Conflict Effectively*. Sage Publications, 2001.

Takaku, Seiji. "The effects of apology and perspective taking on interpersonal forgiveness,"

Journal of Social Psychology, 141(4), 494–508, 2001.

Valerio, Anne Marie and Robert J. Lee. *Executive Coaching: A Guide to the HR Professional*. Pfeiffer, 2004.

Wilmot, William and Joyce Hocker. *Interpersonal Conflict*. New York: McGraw-Hill, 2001.

Yarn, Douglas H., ed. "Conflict Consulting." *Dictionary of Conflict Resolution*. San Francisco: Jossey-Bass Inc., 1999.

Monk, Gerald, and John Winslade. *Practicing Narrative Mediation*. Jossey-Bass, 2008.

Wehr, Paul. *Conflict Regulation*. Boulder, CO: Westview, 1979.

"Conflict Mapping," Burgess, Guy/Burgess, Heidi (eds.). *Beyond Intractability*, Conflict Research Consortium, University of Colorado, Boulder. Posted: September 2006. http://www.beyondintractability.org/essay/conflict_mapping.

Warren, Suzanne and Rod Windle. The National Center on Dispute Resolution in Special Education, www.directionservice.org/cadre/index.cfm.

Websites

http://www.crinfo.org/CK_Essays/ck_iu_messages.jsp

http://www.learningtoforgive.com

http://www.legaldefinition.us/mediation.html

http://www.mediate.com/articles/rundeC3.cfm.

http://www.narrative-meMediation.crinfo.org/

http://www.only-effective-communication-skills.com/imessages

http://www.pbs.org/kqed/onenight/stories/forgive/index.html

http://www.thecoaches.com (Coaches Training Institute)

Other Resources for Conflict Resolution Consultants

Appreciative Coaching: A Positive Process for Change. Sara L. Orem, Jacqueline Binkert, and Ann L. Clancy. Jossey-Bass, 2007.

This book applies the appreciative inquiry method to coaching. Based on various coaching research and tests, the stages of appreciative inquiry are used to create a new coaching methodology. The goal is to help participants become self-aware advocates doing their utmost to achieve their own goals. The book reads like a story, and first tells actual stories of this transformation, followed by the principles of the methodology and real-life examples of those principles, going on to give a concrete outline for the process, and concluding with more details on each of the four stages.

Appreciative Inquiry: A Positive Revolution in Change. David L. Cooperrider and Diana Whitney. Berrett-Koehler Publishers, 2005.

This seems mainly geared toward business and other organizational leaders as a "new model of change management." Essentially, it describes a new approach to problem solving called "appreciative inquiry," which is about the coevolutionary search for the best in people, their organizations, and the relevant world around them.

Assessment for Learning: Putting It into Practice. Paul Black, Chris Harrison, Clare Lee, Bethan Marshall, and Dylan Wiliam. Open University Press, 2003.

This book describes how assessing children for learning during their academic journey can provide great dividends for the educational experience.

Becoming a Conflict Competent Leader. Craig E. Runde and Tim A. Flanagan. San Francisco, CA: Jossey-Bass Business Management Series and the Center for Creative Leadership, 2007.

As they state, more of a leadership book that deals with conflict management than a text on conflict management. The authors openly suggest reading other books to learn explicitly about conflict management. The book seems largely academic, though it has some pragmatic ideas and suggestions.

Bridging Troubled Waters: Conflict Resolution From the Heart. Michelle LeBaron. Jossey-Bass, 2002.

This book describes how to find resolution and/or healing during the conflict process. It is realistic in that it takes into account uncooperative parties, how a win-win scenario is not always available, and what the next-best options are in this circumstance. This book has good messages about understanding and emphasizing with the viewpoint of those we are having the conflict with. However, the book is somewhat wordy, and spends a lot of time telling back stories and quoting various world views. This makes the book interesting, but also makes for a long read to get to the various points and strategies.

Communicating Emotion: Social, Moral, and Cultural Processes. Sally Planalp, Cambridge University Press, 1999.

An in-depth study of the how, what, and why of emotions, this book explores the true nature of the marriage between emotion and communication, and how new research and studies in various disciplines can show the true nature of emotion.

"Communication and Interpersonal Conflict in Organizations." Linda J. Putnam, *Management Communication Quarterly*, Vol. 1(3): 293, 1988.

This academic and difficult to digest article discusses measuring conflict more than combating it.

Communication, Conflict, and the Management of Differences. Stephen W. Littlejohn and Kathy Domenici. Waveland Press, Inc., 2007.

Written from the experience of mediation, this book has both practical tools and academic theories for understanding why conflict occurs and for using communication to stop the downward spiral. Theories it references are not entirely fleshed out, making for a somewhat incomplete reading. Much of the worth of this book might be in its appendix, which lists practical information on conversing through conflicts.

Dynamic Relationships: Unleashing the Power of Appreciative Inquiry in Daily Living. Jacqueline Stavos and Cheri Torres. Taos Institute Publishing, 2005.

This book applies the appreciative inquiry paradigm to one's personal life. Easily readable, it leaves behind complex concepts and research and instead turns that into easy-to-understand language and exercises to be used in everyday life.

Enhancing Learning Through Self-Assessment. David Boud. Routledge, 1995.

While discussing the merits and downfalls of self-assessment in higher education, this book examines concerns about self-assessment within the context of innovative teaching and learning practices.

Executive Coaching: A Guide for the HR Professional. Anna Marie Valerio and Robert J. Lee. Pfeiffer, 2004.

This book highlights cultural/diversity issues, sample plans, and a step-by-step coaching process, but the majority of the book offers background into the nature of a conflict itself.

Handbook of Practical Program Evaluation. Joseph S. Wholey, Harry P. Hatry, and Kathryn E. Newcomer. Jossey-Bass, 1994.

This handbook, though not too useful in conflict management situations, seems the most comprehensive of the others noted. It describes efficient and economical ways of evaluating all types of organizations, from schools to governments to nonprofits.

Hidden Conflict in Organizations: Uncovering Behind-the-Scenes Disputes. Deborah M. Kolb and Jean M. Bartunek. Sage Publications, 1991.

This book studies and describes how conflicts most often arise within organizations over daily routines, especially when considering private and informal conflicts that are commonly handled irrationally. Providing an analyses of how various factors like beer and sexism can fuel conflict, it's an intriguing read, perhaps more enlightening than educational.

How People Negotiate: Resolving Disputes in Different Cultures. Guy Faure. Springer, 2003.

One precept this book sets forth is that a prerequisite to a successful negotiation is acknowledging that different heritages are important in creating character. The author gives examples of differences between cultures, especially when it comes to conflict, and especially in comparison to our Western views. However, at least as much time is spent talking about histories and theories as giving practical suggestions for dealing with situations.

Identity Conflicts: Can Violence be Regulated? J. Craig Jenkin and Esther E. Gottlieb. Transaction Publishers, 2007.

A treatise studying various violent international conflicts, this book analyzes which regulation schemes worked and which did not, and why, and what the best path forward for trying to stop international violent conflicts would be.

Identity Development: Adolescence Through Adulthood. Jane Kroger. Sage Publications, 2007.

Providing an academic description of the formation and evolution of the notion of self through various stages in a person's life, the book also describes how various biological, psychological, and socioeconomic factors can change a person's thoughts on self.

Interpersonal Communication Through the Life Span. Tricia S. Jones, Martin S. Remland, and Rebecca Sanford. Allyn & Bacon, 2006.

This somewhat academic-heavy book highlights new research from psychology and sociology on life as viewed during four phases (through middle childhood, to young adult, to middle adult, and late life); it discusses how to communicate through the main issues of life's stages (i.e., conflict competence, identity, marriage, and grandparenting, respectively).

Law, Culture, and Ritual. Oscar G Chase. NYU Press Academic, 2005.

A book that explores the connection between cultures and dispute resolution, it lays out theories and gives new definitions. While it would appear to provide real insights, it is largely a theory-based book and not a practice-based book. It reads like a good sociology textbook.

Managing Intercultural Conflict Effectively. Stella Ting-Toomey and John Oetzel. Sage Publications, 2001.

Conflict resolution styles for both individualistic and collectivistic individuals are discussed. The book is academic and theoretical, but has fairly practical advice, especially for cross-cultural conflict. Practical parts need to be weeded out from interesting but ultimately unimportant facts and background, however.

Meta-emotion: How Families Communicate Emotionally. John Mordechai Gottman, Lynn Fainsilber Katz, and Carole Hooven. Psychology Press, 1997.

This book tells of research on how families currently interact and what this means for the physical and mental state of the members. The book then sets forth a theory for the best way to interact with family, various ways of interacting that have been purposefully enacted, and their ensuing results.

Negotiation. Roy J. Lewicki, David Saunders, and Bruce Barry. McGraw-Hill/Irwin, 2009.

This academic book, which is highly cited and researched, starts out with a quite valuable chapter describing strategy and tactics of negotiating.

New Directions in Mediation. Joseph P. Folger and Tricia S. Jones. Sage Publications, 1994.

This is an interesting analysis of mediation with suggestions on remaining impartial and maximizing the effectiveness of mediators. It also includes tips on training mediators. Most interesting was its discussion of how socioeconomic views of society and the parties involved impact a mediation. General conflict solving for the parties involved in the conflict was minimal, however.

Nonverbal Communication in Everyday Life. Martin S. Remland. Allyn & Bacon, 2008.

This book describes the concepts and functions of nonverbal communication, ending with a narrative of the skills necessary to master communicating, reading, and reacting to communication. It is written to be readable and accessible to the general public.

Power and Influence in Organizations. Roderick M. Kramer and Margaret A Neale. Sage Publications, 1998.

This is a book compiling the knowledge of many leading experts in the field of organizational relations meshed with the knowledge of up-and-coming scholars in the same areas, analyzing such things as how to appropriately create task teams and attacking sexism and other discrimination.

Pragmatics of Human Communication: A Study of Interactional Patterns, Pathologies, and Paradoxes. Paul Watzlawick, Janet Helmick Beavin, MD, Don D. Jackson. W.W. Norton & Company, 1967.

Highly academic but also highly readable, this book presents basic principles of communication between individuals, and is both existential and practical in terms of addressing problems and dealing with reality.

Program Evaluation, Alternative Approaches and Practical Guidelines. Jody L. Fitzpatrick, James R. Sanders, and Blaine R. Worthen. Allyn & Bacon, 2003.

Most likely not particularly helpful in conflict management, this book describes the majority of modern evaluation processes used for schools and other organizations.

Psychology for Leaders: Using Motivation, Conflict, and Power to Manage More Effectively. Dean Tjosvold and Mary M. Tjosvold. Wiley, 1995.

Largely geared toward business, this is a book full of insights on how leaders can use various tools of psychology to create a shared vision and encourage cooperation, and how to deal with power and emotion.

Relationship Conflict: Conflict in Parent-Child, Friendship, and Romantic Relationships. Dan Canary, William R. Cupach, and Susan J, Messman. Sage, 1995.

This book is as much about studying and defining conflict as it is about solving it. It divides potential conflicts into those between parent and child, between peers (and most importantly friends), and between significant others. It offers many statistics and analyses on conflict, but not much on methods for helping solve conflict. Much more theory based than practice based.

Storytelling in Organizations: Why Storytelling Is Transforming 21st Century Organizations and Management. John Seely, Stephen Denning, Katalina Groh, and Lauren Prusak. Elsevier Butterworth-Heinemann, 2005.

This well-written, interesting book presents the argument that the ability to successfully tell the narrative of events can massively impact events, and offers tips on how to become a better narrator.

Tales for Change: Using Storytelling to Develop People and Organizations. Margaret Parkin. Kogan Page Publishers, 2004.

This interesting book is a collection of tales, like *Aesop's Fables*, with lessons on how storytelling can improve various facets of life, including leadership, emotional intelligence, the stress of change, etc.

The Development of Emotional Competence. Carolyn Saarni. The Guilford Press, 1999.

This book is part academic and part practical, dissecting how emotional competence forms, the importance of emotional competence, and the ways in which people can fully take charge of their own emotional competence or, on a somewhat lesser level, how to be purposeful in promoting the emotional competence of others. It outlines eight different strategies helpful in achieving emotional competence, how they will help, and how to achieve them.

The Handbook of Dispute Resolution. Michael L. Moffitt and Robert C. Bordone. Jossey-Bass, 2005.

A fantastic, practitioner-focused book bringing together many of the most well-regarded theories available, it assumes the reader has no background in the field, yet it has enough new information to be useful to a veteran in the field. Though massive, the book's individual chapters are topical and meant to be fully readable and understandable by themselves. Some of the chapters are highly academic, while others are more practical, depending upon the subject of the chapter.

The Relationship Cure: A 5-Step Guide to Strengthening Your Marriage, Family, and Friendships. John M. Gottman. Three Rivers Press, 2002.

A straightforward and direct book outlining a five-step approach toward saving/helping a romantic relationship.

The Resolution of Conflict: Constructive and Deconstructive Processes. Morton. London: Yale University Press, 1973.

A highly theoretical book on the study of conflict, it identifies good/bad conflicts, potential variables of conflicts, whether the conflict is cooperative or competitive, etc. It concludes with a final essay, which offers some good insight.

The Saturated Self: Dilemmas of Identity in Contemporary Life. Kenneth Gergen. Basic Books, 1991.

This book examines the notion that how we see ourselves impacts our relationships, and discusses how our self-perception is changing with technological advancements.

The Shadow Negotiation. Deborah M. Kolb and Judith Williams. Simon and Schuster, 2001.

Arguing that people are not born negotiators but made into negotiators, the book outlines specifically how women can achieve their maximum potential in this regard. Very readable, not very academic, but instead teaches through stories.

Transcend and Transform: An Introduction to Conflict Work. Johan Galtung. Paradigm Publishers, 2004.

This handbook describes how to deal with all sorts of conflicts, from daily interpersonal conflicts all the way to international conflicts. It offers tips and advice, but also describes conflict theory at length.

What Every Teacher Needs to Know About Assessment. Leslie Walker Wilson, 2004.

While not particularly relevant book for conflict management, this one discusses assessment in the context of No Child Left Behind, and analyzes what are proper and improper roles of assessment in our education system.

Working Through Conflict. Joseph P. Folger, Marshall Scott Poole, and Randall K. Stutman. Harper Collins College Div., 1997.

Somewhat academic but fairly readable, this book focuses on describing well-founded conflict theories and how to apply them. It is a highly analytical book, diving deeply into conflict, describing many potential nuances of conflicts, such as digging into numerous psychological undertones.

Acknowledgments

My thanks to the many people who contributed to the development of the conflict resolution consulting program and to the development of this book, especially Grant Alexis, Jeremy Barthels, Brent Lehman, Mariah Levison, Nick Rogers, Hyrum Salmond, Jessie Shiffman, Randy Victor, and Brian Welle. The development of the Conflict Consulting Program and this book would not have been possible without the generous support of the JAMS Foundation.

About the Author

Karmit J. Bulman is executive director of the Conflict Resolution Center (CRC) in Minneapolis, Minnesota, and an attorney, qualified mediator, and adjunct professor of law at University of Minnesota School of Law. She is a local and national trainer and consultant in the areas of conflict resolution, mediation, communication skills, leadership, organizational development, and fundraising; serves as vice chair of the National Association for Community Mediation; on the leadership team of the Community Section of the Association for Conflict Resolution; and has been the director of nonprofit organizations since 1990.

CRC is a community-based, nonprofit organization formed in 1981 for the purpose of bringing people together to find lasting and effective solutions to conflict. To learn more about the Conflict Resolution Center, visit www.crcminnesota.org, or call 612-822-9883. Information about community mediation and conflict resolution is also available at the National Association for Community Mediation, www.nafcm.org.